AND THAT WAS...
Derek Davis

Derek Davis joined RTÉ as a freelance journalist in 1973 and was staffed as a senior reporter in 1974. He won two prestigious Jacobs' awards as a newscaster and programme presenter.

No one has presented the variety of programmes he has – from hard-nosed news and current affairs to light entertainment. His own passions for fishing, boating, fine food and wine are well known, and he has made scores of programmes on these themes for RTÉ and the BBC.

He lives in Dublin with his wife, a teacher, and his three adult sons. His enthusiasms are not confined to the airwaves, and he is regarded as a very good angler – at sea or on fresh water – and a fine cook.

AND THAT WAS...
Derek Davis

Derek Davis

THE O'BRIEN PRESS
DUBLIN

PUBLISHED IN ASSOCIATION WITH RTÉ

First published 2007 by The O'Brien Press Ltd,
12 Terenure Road East, Rathgar, Dublin 6, Ireland.
Tel: +353 1 4923333; Fax: +353 1 4922777
E-mail: books@obrien.ie
Website: www.obrien.ie

ISBN: 978-1-84717-057-6

Author picture by Beta Bajgartova, courtesy of *TVNow Magazine*

British Library Cataloguing-in-Publication Data
Davis, Derek
And that was Derek Davis
1. Ireland - Social conditions - 21st century
I. Title
306'.09415

1 2 3 4 5 6 7 8 9 10
07 08 09 10 11 12

Typesetting, editing, layout and design: The O'Brien Press Ltd
Printing: Cox and Wyman Ltd.

Contents

Introduction

As broadcasters, most of what we make are ephemera –
like the mayfly, they live for a day in the air and then
vanish. Barring a court case or one of those historical
raids on the tape library for a programme years hence,
our work is done and gone in a day or so. I've been a
maker of ephemera for nearly forty years without ever
publishing a word of a script. I never considered it. It
wasn't modesty, I just never thought of it, and no pub-
lisher ever asked before. This collection is different. It
has been edited and shaped for publication to make it
readable by someone other than me.

The radio columns were commissioned by RTÉ Radio
1's *Five Seven Live* and later *Drivetime* programmes. The
first thing I had to do was to focus on the target audience.
The transmission time meant that a lot of listeners were
commuters, so I assumed the brief of speaking to and for
them. Thousands of tired people on a long, frustrating
odyssey to get home are isolated. I wanted to voice their
frustrations, inform their insecurities and franchise them
to be angry. They are not a few cranky individuals but
part of Ireland's most persecuted and exploited sections
of society: tired, taxed, ill served. Many of the columns
were written for and about them. Data will change from
column to column, as it was updated or superseded by
new information, but not so much that you won't recognise the ongoing lack of honest 'joined-up thinking'.

After four decades of bombardment by spin doctors
and PR practitioners, I'm still amazed at the amount of
pure humbug to which we're subjected. Some of it, like

the anti-litter or anti-smoking campaigns, is in a good cause, but it's still humbug, and it sticks in my craw.

It's not my function to précis press releases but to examine them carefully so that when a well-funded quango claims huge success after the smoking ban, we want it to be true, but then the revenue figures show an 8-per-cent increase in tobacco sales before any price increase. At that point, we know that all the great claims were just smoke. I've come under pressure by criticising sacred cows but no challenge has stood up to scrutiny so far.

There's a group of columns, written over a period of about three years, that deal with events in Northern Ireland, and I don't pretend to be detached. Horror and fear shaped my views over a long period, and I rejoice at eventually being wrong on one key issue. I never believed that the Ian Paisley I watched all my adult life would ever share power with Catholics, let alone Republicans. I'm still shocked. This was a conversion to make Saint Paul's look like a modest change of lifestyle. I'm still, at the time of writing, elated and hugely optimistic. Will it last?

We've also compiled a section on the changes in Irish life over the years, witnessed by this journalist over a long period. With that came the realisation that my own working life was rapidly approaching an end – even life itself. I was getting old. I can cope, so far, with becoming a curmudgeon, wearing beige and getting more closely acquainted with members of the medical profession. What frightens me is the low priority of the elderly in our national esteem and within the state systems. It starts when shop assistants ignore you and maybe ends completely neglected in a nursing home. Change it now, while you can.

I don't propose that this collection be regarded as great literature, but I hope it will, at times, provoke, inform, amuse or just divert the reader. There was a nineteenth-century wit, the Revd Sidney Smith, an Anglican vicar who never rose above that rank in the Church of England while a stern, humourless relative became a bishop. When asked to explain the difference in their careers, Sidney observed that while his relative rose through gravity, he, Sidney, had sunk through levity. I have some fellow feeling for the poor Revd Sid, but, I promise you, the intention of the columns was serious if at times an irritating flippancy creeps in. Sorry, it's just the way I am – old dog, new tricks.

After this ramble, there's a short, selective and self-serving biography. My editor pointed out that, like mumps and salmonella, mine was a household name, so people know who I am but little about me. It would be a lot less embarrassing if I wrote a few lines on my peculiar lineage and development before someone else did something more revealing. I've kept it short.

Outside the Tribe

It is very, very hard to be impartial. Most of us not only have opinions but also loyalties to our tribe and its codes of conduct. These loyalties are enforced by a fear of rejection or ejection from the tribe. For example, it is very tough for a Protestant nationalist in Northern Ireland to be fully accepted by either side, and a Roman Catholic unionist will also feel the chill of tribal rejection. In the Irish Republic, it is still easier not to rock the boat, to go with the consensus, to be at all times politically correct and, publicly, at least, to embrace the beliefs of our neighbours and masters.

These beliefs change. At one time, it was profitable and career-advancing to the Irish media to be avowedly religious, even to join Opus Dei or the Knights of St Columbanus. If that didn't suit, you could become radical and join the Workers Party. It was always useful to be an Irish-language enthusiast and to flaunt your Gaelic ancestors and credentials, but if none of the above was appropriate, you were outside the main tribe.

There were lesser tribes numerically. You could be from a long Protestant tradition, so long as it wasn't also unionist. You could be a charming and cherished anachronism in a large decaying country house. That made you 'Anglo-Irish' with a bit of a pedigree – so long as you stayed away from politics.

If you didn't fit into any of the established tribes, you enjoyed no tribal benefits. There was no one to vouch for you. Promotion became difficult because managers like to advance those whom they perceive to be in their own image. They talk about diversity and pluralism, but that's all it is – talk about two fine-sounding words.

It's cold outside the tribe. It took me a while to realise that I was born never to be more than on the fringes of any tribe – being a bit bloody-minded hasn't helped. Where organised religion and politics are concerned, I've spent a lot of my life sitting on the fence. It's an uncomfortable position, but the view is spectacular.

My father was a Protestant unionist from Belfast who met my Catholic nationalist mother in her home town of Bray, County Wicklow. After a respectable courtship, they decided to marry. Both of their families had reservations about the match. My mother's father, a former English cavalryman, had converted to Catholicism to marry her mother. My father's mother had converted from Methodist to Church of Ireland to marry his father, but neither of my prospective parents had any intention of converting to anything. Instead, to keep both sides of the family happy, they were married twice! The first wedding was in a so-called chapel of ease in Bray. The union was too shameful to be celebrated in the parish church. The second wedding was in a Church of Ireland church in Belfast. Both sides were satisfied that there was now a valid marriage in the eyes of their God.

When first my sister then I were born, the routine was well established – up the road to get baptised in the

Church of Ireland and, an hour later, down the road to have the whole process repeated in the Roman Catholic Church. Double indemnity.

Education for my sister wasn't a problem. She was sent off daily to a very nice Catholic convent school and then to a very civilised boarding school run by the same order in Ballycastle, County Antrim. Sybil Connolly, the renowned couturière, designed their wardrobe of hats and uniforms. Miss Jean Brodie would have been completely at home there.

My education was another matter. By this time, we were living in Bangor, County Down. The Catholic population was less than 10 per cent of the total 36,000 souls, but it was, for the most part, a friendly, middle-class town, very confident and cosy in its Protestant, unionist ethos. There was a small cadre of hard-core bigots, but they were very short of targets for their bigotry. Bangor was a dormitory town for Belfast and, in the summer, a busy seaside resort. There weren't enough Catholics in Bangor for active discrimination or prejudice in jobs. There was no need for any gerrymandering because a 90-per-cent majority guaranteed the safest of unionist seats. I think my father picked Bangor because, geographically, it was a bit like my mother's home town Bray and because it was relatively free from the tensions found in other parts of the province.

Schools were a problem. Whereas my sister could commute to nearby Holywood to a 'good' Catholic school, I didn't have the same option. The local Catholic primary school wasn't great, and it wasn't handy. I was signed up for a Protestant fee-paying prep school. My father would have preferred that I was raised Church of

Ireland, but my mother prevailed, and these two accomplished compromisers agreed that I would be educated in a Protestant school but sent off to the local Convent of Mercy for religious instruction as a Catholic.

My father's case for Protestantism had little to do with God. His view was that as a Roman Catholic in Northern Ireland I would never be fully accepted into the professions or the upper echelons of the business community. Catholics were, of course, second-class citizens. It wasn't right, but that's the way it was, and he wanted the best for his son.

The compromise meant that during bible studies at school, I stood outside in the corridor while Miss Knox, a skeletal redhead, pinned pictures on a flannel board and told stories about King David, Esau, Moses and loads more. I could hear perfectly well through the closed door, but I missed out on the pictures. Because the school had every shade of Protestant child in attendance, most of Miss Knox's stories were from the Old Testament, thereby avoiding any serious doctrinal differences. The basic story of the New Testament was presented too but with nothing like the wrath-filled detail of the Old Testament.

In contrast, when I trotted off to Mother Paul on Saturday mornings, nearly all the talk was of the New Testament. Adult experience would teach me that thundering Protestant fundamentalists would get much of their inspiration and subject matter from the Old Testament with its vengeful God, and Catholics were, by and large, profoundly ignorant of all but the book of Genesis.

At this stage, I had a fair troupe of pals, all Protestant. They joined the local scouts and the Boys' Brigade through their churches. I was an outsider. There were wonderful beaches and a huge outdoor swimming pool in Bangor, and I could swim like a seal. School holidays were spent in Pickie Pool, but because most of the competitive events were organised through church groups, I was mostly excluded. No one shouted sectarian abuse at me. Our neighbours were decent, God-fearing folk, and, so far as I know, none of my pals was told to avoid me because I was an RC. Yet, I knew I didn't quite fit in. I wasn't a full member of the tribe.

One evening, over dinner, my mother became quite distressed and showed my father a letter she had received from the Roman Catholic Bishop of Down and Connor. In it, he threatened to have her barred from the sacraments if I wasn't sent to a Catholic school. I was immediately angry with this man who had made my mother cry. Even now, I remain indignant because, to the end of her days, she was an extremely devout and diligent Catholic. My father slipped a big arm around her shoulder and said, 'Don't worry love, we'll send him to Garron Tower'.

I knew nothing of this place, but in a few days my father had obtained the school syllabus. It read well. The food was well described, and there was lots of sport. It was also a diocesan seminary, which would endeavour to recruit apprentice priests. To say that the literature overstated the comforts of the school is this year's understatement.

To start with, my accent was all wrong. Most of the pupils had the sharp tones of West Belfast or the Scottish clip of County Antrim. The latter wasn't surprising, since the school was located 300 feet above the Antrim coast road between Carnlough and Cushendall, directly opposite the Mull of Kintyre on the coast of Scotland. On a clear day, it was possible to discern cars moving on the mull. The location was spectacular. Hundreds of feet of hazel-covered hillside rose behind the school to the flat heather land of the Antrim plateau.

My posh prep-school vocabulary earned me the nickname 'Dictionary Davis', and my well-rounded vowels marked me out for ridicule. Add to that a complete ignorance of Gaelic sports, a Protestant father and a weight problem: I was the target of any tormentor in the school. It didn't help that I was extremely passive, had almost never had a fight (the prep school discouraged that sort of thing) and was a complete duffer at maths and science. My school days were miserable.

I learned to play Gaelic football and handball. I came to appreciate the skill of the hurlers and had lots of healthy exercise climbing the hills. I also learned to smoke. Just about everyone except the Head, Fr. Tomelty and three St Louis nuns smoked. Maybe a couple of others abstained, but smoking, for my generation, was a rite of passage that continued into adulthood. It was also part of being 'accepted'. Today, I know that the best way of dealing with the smoking problem is to stop people starting.

The food was pretty grim – prison fare. The nun in charge of the kitchens did her best, but the budget was slender because the fees were relatively low.

Like many schools at the time, there was corporal punishment, but few would have administered it so routinely and so enthusiastically. The regime was quite savage. Severe beatings for the most minor infractions were the norm, and student prefects – sixteen- or seventeen-year-olds – had the power to flog. Bullying was rife. A few gentle souls went home quietly with breakdowns and never returned. The rest of us got tough. I learned not to complain, not to show fear and not to back down. Any weakness would only make life more miserable.

They had an interesting take on religion too. There was, of course, compulsory mass in the mornings and benediction in the evenings, but a change of bishop introduced the innovation of compulsory confession once a month. Perhaps, for me, that was the last straw. Such compulsion was theologically unsound, oppressive and counter-productive. All the time, two strands of life ran together: violence and religion.

A new nun arrived to teach music. She was a pretty and gentle little woman who had been teaching in a convent in County Down. Within a day or two, she was strolling around the playing fields after school as a number of 'house' matches were beginning. Two twelve-year-old boys arrived a few minutes late and were promptly punched unconscious by the priest who was also the referee. I kid you not. I met her running tearfully away from the scene and assured her that this was perfectly normal here. It was too.

She became a great friend who would try, with mixed results, to teach me to sing, would sew on my buttons and repair my torn jacket. She was a sensitive and caring person, completely out of place in that school.

There was a cadre of lay teachers who travelled in every day, and some of them were very good indeed. Almost without exception they lacked the clerical flair for atrocious punishment, perhaps because they were still connected to a more civilised world beyond the school gates.

You may think I'm exaggerating the violence. It really was routine. Once, aged about fifteen, I was comparing Greek homework, leaning out of the third-floor window of my little room. My neighbour suddenly ducked back in, and a voice from below roared, 'Davis, I'm coming up to get you!' Well, I expected a few slaps from the priest who'd caught me talking out the window during study. What I didn't know was that my neighbour on the other side had clocked him with an apple core.

A moment or two later, the priest was outside my door, white with fury and brandishing a heavy cane. One, two, three – after a dozen or so lashes, the cane broke, and he flung it down. As I looked down at the cane, he caught me with a haymaker of a punch between the eyes. My legs went, as my head hit the wall, and I slid down. He didn't stop. He started kicking me in the stomach and the ribs. I was saved by another priest who came running along the corridor shouting, 'Pull yourself together!' He manhandled my assailant away and helped me back into my room.

Nothing more was ever said. I met the man who assaulted me many times since, but never a word of regret or apology.

Six wretched years passed, and then the period to A levels was increased to two years. It was time to move. I went to St Malachy's College in Belfast, a huge school on the Antrim Road. I was, like most there, a day student, commuting from Bangor, about 14 miles each day. It was bliss. We were treated like adults, had an opportunity to meet girls and didn't go around beating up people.

Mind you, old habits die hard. My father caught me with a packet of cigarettes when I was fourteen. He told me I could start smoking when I was earning the money to pay for them myself. It was summer, and I went off and got a part-time job in the Old Inn, located in Crawfordsburn, a quaint little village a few miles from Bangor. It was a little piece of Hampshire created in north County Down.

After a couple of years, I moved to another bar job closer to home. This place, the Sefton Hotel, was next door to a big ballroom. The bouncers, big, confident, hard dandies, would have a drink before going on duty. I got to know them well. One night, they were short-staffed, and I accepted their invitation to join their ranks. My parents didn't know, and my qualifications for the job were based entirely on my size. I was only sixteen, but big. Even my robust boarding-school education didn't equip me for the job of bouncer, but I was a quick learner and would eventually manage a nightclub with another company while pursuing an academic career as a law student and the beginnings of a life in broadcasting.

By the time I was twenty, I'd had experience in the food-and-drink trade, ballrooms, nightclubs, the BBC and Queen's University's Law Faculty. At twenty-one, I'd won all the major debating competitions, the Queen's Orator, the Lord Chief Justice's Prize and, of course, the Fresher's Prize. With partner Brendan Keenan, the Irish Times Trophy followed, and we were individual winners of the Observer Mace, the British intervarsity competition. That year, three students received honorary life memberships of the Student's Union: Brendan Keenan,

Derek Davis and, for entirely different reasons, Bernadette Devlin.

These were fiercely political times, and, in that regard, I was both ignorant and naive. I was never a full member of any of Northern Ireland's opposing tribes. University society was as close to any tribal membership as I came. The unionists' chickens were coming home to roost. The post-war education acts had given free third-level education, grant-aided, to all. A new generation of vociferous, well-educated young nationalists was going through the system. These young men and women, Bernadette Devlin amongst them, were articulate, passionate and persuasive. They focused attention on discrimination, gerrymandering, grievance after grievance. They became the engine room of the civil-rights movement and attracted more than Catholic students. Young Protestants, in large numbers, took part in the early marches.

Bill Craig was the Unionist Minister for Home Affairs. Craig was a tough hardliner. His prime minister Terence O'Neill was an old Etonian and slightly embarrassed by the right wing of his own party. He was also weak. Though he wasn't the last grandee to hold the job of Northern Ireland Prime Minister, there would be another power struggle between the landed gentry and the merchant middle class. This class struggle went almost unrecorded as the bigger story of violence and political polarisation took place. Craig's aggressive response to the civil-rights movement gave it even more impetus, but it wasn't long before the old sectarianism had fractured the North. Young Protestants either rejoined the unionist camp or left the province in despair. Catholics took up traditional positions. Thirty years of chaos have been well catalogued.

Working as a stringer, a low form of freelance life, for ABC, the American company, I saw too much. Some I have worked with enjoy the ability to metabolise the horror and just get on with the job. By the time I was twenty-four, I'd been shot at, blown up, threatened many times and had seen such horror it is difficult now to recall without a shudder. For me, the tragedy and the melancholy were cumulative. I had difficulty sleeping, was depressed and wanted out. I had no place in all of this. I wasn't part of these tribes. When an opportunity, bizarrely, arose to join a showband based in Cork, I seized it, but, of course, I wasn't a musician, sang badly and, after the initial buzz, went back up north. It was grim. I didn't stay long.

Heart trouble had killed my father the morning after his art business in Belfast was bomb-damaged for the fifth time. It would be blown up twice more by republican bombs. Loyalist roadblocks at the time ensured a small turn-out for his funeral, and my mother was now the target for intimidation by loyalist bully boys. A short time later, I moved both of us south to Dublin. We had no place in the North.

The welcome south of the border was a few *fáiltes* short of *céad míle*. This was 1973, the start of the paranoid years, when anyone with a northern accent was an object of suspicion and work was hard to find. Surprisingly, I got a telephone in about ten days – unheard of normally, when the waiting time was typically six months. A streetwise friend explained, 'If you don't have a phone, they can't tap it. It helps if you're from the North.'

I felt very isolated. I had no circle of friends, wasn't a fugitive republican and spoke no Irish. A lot of doors were closed. There was an unlikely snobbery as well. A year in a showband to some was like the mark of Cain – no wonder a senior NUJ officer would describe me and a cameraman I worked with as 'undesirables'. The Dublin freelance branch was starting, and I joined the union through it. Subsequently, I helped others, like Eamon Dunphy, get their NUJ card, which, no matter what anyone tells you, is a very necessary item in a reporter's wallet.

I'd shared a flat briefly, as a student, with Tom McGurk, and he was one of the few people I knew in Dublin. We were enjoying a modest dinner in his basement flat in Waterloo Road when the Head of News at RTÉ phoned. The Night Editor had suffered a heart attack, could he (McGurk) possibly look after the newsroom overnight? Tom was already scheduled to prepare and present *It Says in the Papers* and couldn't do both, but he told the caller, Wesley Boyd, that he had a distinguished northern journalist dining with him – me! Wesley was desperate enough to give me a try, and I became the £12.50-a-night editor of everything from 11pm to 6.30am. It worked out.

By September 1974, I had three job offers: a contract from BBC; a staff job as a senior reporter on the RTÉ news desk; and the role of the narrator in Noel Pearson's production of *Joseph and the Amazing Technicolor Dreamcoat.* I took the RTÉ gig. At last, I'd found a tribe – or so I thought. I'd just missed some of the subtleties. I had a mentor, a brilliant and shrewd news editor called Barney Cavanagh. There were others too, but my social circle was, and remains, quite small. The job wasn't my life, and when the tribe met to swallow pints or play golf,

I was hardly ever there. It was my choice not to become a courtier, and I've never had an easy relationship with the powerful. Never show fear, never show weakness – old habits too easily construed as a lack of respect. Most of my close friends, not all, are outside journalism and broadcasting, and I've learnt more about what's happening in the real world from them than from all the late-night drinking sessions with colleagues.

The view from outside the tribe is seen through a wide angle; yes, the position on the fence remains uncomfortable, but the view is still so much better. I have personal loyalties and affections, but they're not tribal, and the radio columns, many of them reproduced here, are written from that perspective. I'm becoming less tolerant of humbug, shirkers, posers and other chancers. But then, I was never known for grabbing the forelock.

Hectored by Bureaucrats

My tolerance for spin has decreased dramatically. Most of the spinners are former journalists, and though some have a good pedigree, others were chancers and bluffers as journalists; they haven't mended their ways now, earning huge chunks of public cash. I really don't care that they've fallen on their feet, but there is evidence that they've become a block to proper grass-roots feedback, and, worse, they've sinned against logic and reason. They've dreamt up quick fixes and photo ops to give their minister profile.

What's the harm? When road-safety thinking is all hunch and spin, people will die. When decisions are taken in Health, these can affect everyone's lives. Garda deployment, crime figures and the suchlike all affect us. Beware spin and those who practise it.

The greatest compliment I've received is the letter from the spin doctor to the Director General seeking to silence me. Yeah, I know about that. I've railed against the system in child-abuse cases, the lack of real long-term management of roads and lots more. The following section is a number of thoughts on a variety of subjects.

Spin it like candyfloss, pal

Broadcast 27 September 2004

Anyone who remembers the British television series *Yes Minister* will recall the manipulative power of senior civil servants, but there was another character who turned up from time to time; he was the political adviser, a shrewd assessor of the political impact of the Minister's actions or his inactivity. Now, although that series was a caricature of political life, most insiders, including Mrs Thatcher, it is interesting to note, reckoned that it was painfully close to the truth. A political adviser is the eyes and ears of the minister in the real world – long-range radar, if you like – and a good one is brutally frank! But ministerial egos are at least as large as those of broadcasters.

In Ireland, the backbenchers were, for generations, the early warning system, along with the trusted constituency agent. But something strange happened over the past few years. The number of spin doctors increased; the fees paid to PR companies grew; and grass-roots feedback didn't seem to be getting through. Ministers appeared to believe that good spinning and their own eloquence could make everything right when, if they had listened to the grass roots, there would have been very little need for repair or rescue.

It was this broadcaster on *Five Seven Live* who, as far as I know, first questioned on air the implementation of the penalty-points system. It was, I admit, not rocket science, simply the result of being sent to the four corners of Ireland to talk to its citizens and then doing a bit of elementary spadework. I was able to confirm that only a very tiny percentage of serious accidents occurred on our motorways and dual carriageways, the best roads. That figure is now accepted to be just 3 per cent. Indeed, the busiest road in the country, the M50, has recorded, as far as I know, not a single fatality this year. But about 84 per cent of policing is on those, the safest roads in the country. The official response was at first to say that, 'Oh no, 40 per cent of serious accidents were on our main roads.' That was a subtle change of definition. We have lots of lethal stretches of main road, twisting two-lane shameful tracks. But those dual carriageways and motorways, no: just 3 per cent of serious accidents.

So Séamus Brennan had come up with a penalty-points system with a great potential to save lives. But, its implementation (in fairness, not his department) has brought the system into disrepute, failed to curb the deaths and caused a great deal of hostility towards both the Government and the Gardaí. If the Government listened to its grass roots, they would know that.

A huge number of gardaí, we are told, are scared at work, often patrolling on foot alone or holding the fort in an otherwise-deserted garda station. Well, I have to tell you that many ordinary citizens are also scared on the streets and in their homes because they have no faith that the Gardaí will turn up at all when called. Daylight attacks on main streets are a particular cause of anger when so much manpower is out on the dual carriageways catching those who stray over often-unrealistic limits.

The citizens believe that garda priorities are wrong, that its management is shambolic. The 2,000 extra gardaí promised just never appeared, but the most stinging criticism from the citizen is that existing resources are mismanaged. How many able-bodied gardaí are pushing pens, delivering summons, collecting fines when we want to see them on the streets? Their lonely colleagues want to see them on the streets.

What happened to the idea of an auxiliary constabulary, the part-time reservists acting under the supervision of a full-time garda, men and women who know the problems of their area or who could do some of those administrative tasks?[1]

As it is, the citizen believes that the priorities are wrong, that the Gardaí are expected to catch a quota of speeding motorists and not to prevent accidents on dangerous stretches of road, where most of those accidents occur but where, indeed, most sane and sober drivers actually drive with great care.

The citizen and the ordinary garda want more protection from crime. You can spin that story like candyfloss, pal, but that's the truth. Does anybody believe that we will see 2,000 extra gardaí, not replacement gardaí, *extra* gardaí, within the lifetime of this government? I'm told that Templemore couldn't supply those numbers in that time frame anyway. And yet, that promise stands.

1 Michael McDowell drove on the idea against stiff opposition, especially from the Garda Representative Association. To date, only a small number of recruits has appeared on the streets. It's not yet known if the new minister has the same enthusiasm.

The Government doesn't need think tanks, it needs to listen. We hear about recommendations to put up the price of alcohol – oh, the dope dealers would just love that – and plans to shut down nightclubs early. That appeared in some of the Sunday newspapers. Well, if all that is true, it means more odium for the Government, especially from the under-thirties. And why? Because it is not fair. Why punish everyone for the sins of a few? Punish the drunk, not the innocent drinker. Find some gardaí somewhere and arrest violent thugs. Let the young boogie all night if they want to; it's part of being young and being free.

Australia tackled drinking and driving with random breath-testing and public drunkenness with huge fines for both the drunk and the supplier of the drink. There are 'drunk tanks' to receive the inebriated, keeping their admission to casualty units well down. When the National Roads Authority – remember that, the *National Roads Authority* – complains that some speed limits are preposterously low, as at the Glen o' the Downs in Wicklow, someone really should listen to them. Speed limits that are too low on motorway-quality road undermine the credibility of the whole speed-limit system.

Experts say that our learner drivers need more and better training. Between a quarter and a third of all our drivers are on provisional licences, no argument. But we are promised new rules without sensibly reassessing a training system and a practical test which are more than thirty years out of date. And by the way, relatively few serious accidents involve learner drivers. No, a disproportionate number of serious accidents involve young males late at night or in the early hours of the morning.

Some may, indeed, be suicides. Some are quite probably drug-related, but the Gardaí have little ability to test for recreational drugs. Such tests do exist, but we don't have them. And anyway, who is listening?

Closed ranks

Broadcast 30 October 2005

Even in these well-informed days, when we are almost unshockable, the report on clerical abuse in the diocese of Ferns makes truly awful reading. It's not just that abuse occurred, but how it was protected. The principal institutions did more than just fail by omission but took decisions to protect the criminal and disadvantage the victim. It's an insight into how what could be called 'the Establishment' closed ranks.

More than thirty years ago, I was on my way into RTÉ to work the overnight shift on the news desk. An oncoming car on a stretch of road, narrowed by roadworks, cut a deep furrow in the side of my car. I got out; so did the other driver. He was very obviously drunk as a skunk, a middle-aged man, well dressed, in an expensive car, but very, very drunk. We were blocking the road, and he suggested that we move the cars and then exchange details. Still, for whatever reason, I noted his car number plate. He got back into his car and drove off like blazes. No mobile phones in those days, so I had to find a telephone box and call the local Gardaí. They identified the driver as a prominent medical man with garda connections. 'What do you intend to do?' I asked. 'Absolutely nothing', came the reply, and the garda hung up. I was used to prominent people having an edge with the Police, but even in the North at that time, an MP's wife failed to get a drunk-in-charge summons quashed. There were limits there, but I wondered how many well-placed alcoholics got away with drunken driving here because the Gardaí turned a blind eye? And what else did the powerful get away with?

Ferns has confirmed our worst fears. Theoretically, of course, no one is above the law, but generations of politicians have been happy to turn up for photo calls with the clergy at the opening of schools and other civic events. It was respectability by association, being seen on the side of the angels – no votes in staying away. The church-gate collection remains an important thing to some parties, and, in the run-up to an election, the after-mass hustings guarantee a good crowd. On the face of it, no great harm.

The Roman Catholic Church was seen as the cement that held this state together. For all the physical and sexual abuse that occurred, there was also a huge volume of good work done by good clerics. Priests, nuns and brothers provided most of the education here at a time when we couldn't afford anything else, and some of the caring institutions really did care.

I remember the anger of a young priest I met fishing the river Slaney, in County Wexford. They – he and his colleagues – had known of the abuse and the abusers, but no one would listen to them. Ordinary, decent priests now felt that they were all being tarred with the same filthy brush. Key to the protection from prosecution of the offenders was the garda response. I believe that in a lot of minor offences, the Gardaí should have the discretion to prosecute or not, but in the case of a serious indictable offence, what they used to call a felony, this cannot be the case.

There is a problem. Every promotion above the rank of inspector is a cabinet appointment, and every garda knows that. An ambitious garda knows that he or she must keep the politicians on side. Rank-and-file gardaí know that they must keep their senior officers on side. The politicians know that, at least in the past, it paid to have a good relationship with the Diocese. So the temptation must have existed to protect the offender and his institution, the Church, even at the expense of the victim. Men who should have been locked up were not properly investigated and, therefore, free to reoffend.

It's not just in the area of sex abuse that strange things happen to investigations. The Dublin bombings investigation was wrapped up with unseemly haste. The best-qualified gardaí were kept away from it, and, of course, the files went missing. The murder of a man called Seamus Ludlow outside Dundalk was investigated by a very good detective who was then ordered to close down the investigation. The suspicion of political interference persists. The politicians must relinquish their ability to exert undue influence over the Gardaí – the ability to grant what amounts to immunity to abusers, even murderers – but, of course, they won't. The bishops persecuted, destroyed, the career of the Senior Dean of St Patrick's College, Maynooth because he complained about the inappropriate behaviour of another senior cleric. The politicians retain the power to destroy the career of a garda who rocks the boat. So who is there to protect society? The media, that's who. Lord knows, we're not perfect, but we're all you've got.

A plea for joined-up thinking
Broadcast 11 November 2005

I've whinged for a long time about the lack of real long-term transport planning – the kind of thing that we have seen for years: roads which are inadequate for traffic volume almost before they are completed. The reasons that you are sitting in a traffic jam twice a day are manifold.

It starts with a lack of vision, but it is rooted in our administration system whereby the very senior people, up to and including ministers, know that they will be long gone from office before the perfectly foreseeable problems will become acute. Meanwhile, of course, the books balance. The last bit of the M50 motorway opened only in the last year, still just two lanes each way and, of course, nicely bottlenecked at one end by those wretched toll-booths, a limitless gold mine for the owners. The southern ring road around Cork City hits the Kinsale roundabout, which could have had a flyover from the time of construction, which is now getting one after years of congestion and at huge additional cost.

Gorey, Enniscorthy, New Ross, Waterford, Mitchelstown, Fermoy, towns like Loughrea and, indeed, many other spots west: we've known for years that bypass roads were essential, not optional. Some are works in progress, others still under discussion. Bypassed towns prosper. They are better places in which to live, and safer too.

I suppose I should stop whinging now that something resembling a plan has been announced by the Government. Thirty-four billion euro, or thereabouts, worth of projects and, indeed, a senior academic apparently appointed to oversee them. But a lot of the detail is still a mystery. The north-west remains a separate remote state and, to an extent, so does the south-west.

It's not just the comfort of your commute we are talking about; there are many other national issues inextricably linked to transport infrastructure. It's now officially recognised that bad roads kill. Relatively few fatalities occur on our best roads, so good infrastructure saves lives.

Property values in metropolitan areas are artificially high because the alternative is that gruelling daily journey on overcrowded public transport or congested roads. Paradoxically, those house prices force more and more to join the sprawl out of town, but, because the infrastructure is poor, investment in job creation remains concentrated in and around the cities.

Child-minding surfaced in the last by-elections as a serious election issue and, not surprisingly, because those constituencies have thousands of long-haul commuters who might spend four hours or more every single day trying to get from home to work and back again. Good infrastructure won't solve the problem, but it will alleviate it.

And then there is the location of A&E units in acute hospitals. It's disingenuous to reassure people that there is an A&E unit just 20 or 30 miles away. It's not distance that matters, it's time. If a victim has to wait an inordinate length of time for an ambulance to fight its way through our traffic, the result can be fatal. Not the fault of the

Health Service; that's the failure of the infrastructure. Bad roads also affect already poor garda-response times.

There is a strong anti-car lobby in some quarters, dark mutterings about congestion charges and the perceived success of such charges in London. Well, they *have* helped in a city very well served by public transport, but most Irish commuters don't have a realistic choice, so such charges at the moment would merely be a nasty bit of politically correct dogma – a fact, you will be relieved to note, acknowledged by the Minister this week. But beware, they are out there.

Opposition spokespersons have been at pains to point out that the infrastructural plan is very short of detail, even to the point of being puzzling. A metro line from somewhere near Tallaght to the airport. Could that be a preparatory step for a second airport in west Dublin? A metro line linking the two airports? It *would* make sense.

What about the provision of services on our new roads? The Minister told the National Roads Authority to reconsider their decision (that, by the way, means reverse it) not to make provisions for services, rest areas, toilets and so on – not surprisingly, since the latest thinking indicates that driver fatigue is just as dangerous as excessive alcohol use. So, let us join up these two bits of thinking and start building service areas.

The appearance of an outline plan must not be an end to thinking. For example, why do ferry companies disgorge fleets of trucks into the middle of the morning rush hour? Not an hour earlier, not an hour later, but right at the height of the morning madness. Of course, you can hear the bureaucrat's response, 'Sorry, that's not my department.'

Is there any such thing as a free lunch?

Broadcast 19 December 2005

I received an unsolicited Christmas gift the other day: some wine, very good wine, not hugely expensive but very good. It was a present from a vineyard owner who featured on a programme I presented a few weeks ago. No, Your Worship, it was not a quid pro quo, there was no deal done, it was quite simply an unsolicited gift. Journalists, of course, have no register of members' interests, as politicians do. That's not to say that there aren't rules. Take a bribe in cash or kind to publish or not to publish something; if proven, expect to lose your job or, at least, your reputation.

Fortunately, perhaps, I was only once offered a bribe, and it was resistibly small: a cheque from a showband manager was tucked into my breast pocket. We had just booked his act for a television show; he thought it was the done thing. I didn't make a fuss, I just returned it and assured him that we only booked acts on their merits. But where does one draw the line on food and drink, hospitality? Famously in Dublin journalism, the reporter who most frequently used the phrase 'There is no such thing as a free lunch' became a PR man and, in the 1970s, dispensed more free lunches than anyone else in town!

Shortly after, I was staffed as a reporter in the RTÉ newsroom; that was early in 1974. I was sent down the road to record some minor happening, I think it was in

B&I.[1] I don't remember the story, just that there was an announcement. I conducted an interview, and we all had tea and chocolate biscuits. As we left, each of us was given a bottle of whiskey by the affable press officer. I thanked him but was a bit uneasy about it, and I sought a quiet word with the boss, the RTÉ Director of News – tough, fair and a very good journalist in his own right. 'Did you get the whiskey before or after you did the interview?' 'Oh, after', I said. 'And you weren't expecting anything?' 'Only tea and biscuits.' The response was a bit Jesuitical, but spot on. He said, 'That's all right then, it didn't influence the way you did the story.' And that was the key: Could a gift realistically influence your journalistic processes?

All around the town to this day – in fact, probably on this very day – PR people are pouring food and drink into journalists on behalf of their clients – in most cases just to prove to the clients that they are doing something for their money. Generally, there is very little advantage to either. In fact, a story or photo opportunity will be judged by a hard-bitten editor or chief sub, but the world is full of temptations. Anyone in charge of purchasing for a big company will get lots of small gifts and occasionally hints at larger ones, and some will succumb to temptation.

Even gardaí have, at times, not been beyond reproach. The highest standards are expected from those dispersing large sums of public money or making decisions that have grave importance. We have enough tribunal

1 The now-defunct shipping line.

evidence to know that sometimes there are low standards in high places. Ivor Callely's 1,500-punt house-painting job was inappropriate because he might have been in a position to help the construction company who picked up the tab. No one can say he did, but it doesn't look right or proper. And if it was an oversight or error of judgement, he has paid a huge price – but rightly so.

What of all those construction contracts, the appallingly bad deals on computer projects and transport systems? You see, there is public indignation about the waste of public money, but there is also widespread public suspicion that no one could be stupid enough to make those deals unless . . . well, there is absolutely no evidence of any wrongdoing, but then there is no transparency; we don't even know who made the deals, or if, following the report of the Controller and Auditor General, someone, anyone, will be censured. There needs to be a very public scrutiny of the process by which billions are spent and very clear ethical guidelines for the protection of the decision-makers themselves and for the reassurance when it all goes pear-shaped that they are merely stupid and incompetent. We can believe that.

Conquistadors of the ocean

Broadcast 27 February 2006

A few years ago, I was filming in Vigo in northern Spain. The fleet there is huge and famous for its secret holds, undersized fish and widespread disregard for any law that comes between it and its fish. The Spanish, who consume, per capita, at least five times as much fish as we do, regard their fishermen as heroes, the new conquistadors of the ocean.

I like the Spanish, even went to night classes to learn a little of the language, but when I attempted to film in the auction room where the fish were on show and on sale, I was told in no uncertain terms that I and my camera crew would be thrown into the harbour – so far, something that hasn't happened in an Irish port.

I'm not unsympathetic to trawlermen; on the contrary, theirs is a difficult and very dangerous trade, driven by the need, in many cases, to serve huge loans. They venture out deep in weather as nauseating as it is perilous. The rewards can be good, the temptation to break the rules great, and the rules themselves can be as complex as they are at times daft.

A trawler must have tonnage; that's the right to catch a certain weight of fish. It's a bit like a farmer with a milk quota. That tonnage is traded for cash, and a fisherman buying a bigger, better, safer, more efficient boat can expect to pay a couple of million euro, at least, for even a modest one and maybe the same again to buy the quota, the tonnage. Then there are national quotas for different species landed, so a skipper has to keep very detailed logbooks ready for inspection at any time. The theory is that this will conserve and manage stocks.

Ireland sold a huge amount of fishing rights to the EU in exchange for cash back in the 1980s. Fishermen always say that the Lucan by-pass was built on mackerel! Our waters weren't wide open to our EU partners, but the rules were wide open to abuse. The white-fish fleet out of Castletownbere, mostly smaller, older timber boats, were at times bullied off their legitimate fishing grounds by big steel boats from southern Europe, and, despite more investment, that fleet still struggles to get a good return. Fewer and fewer young men from the area want to go to sea. East European crews, very competent, are very common now.

Meanwhile, the mackerel fleet in Donegal was investing in bigger and bigger boats. Ten million euro, 15 million, 20 million and climbing, feeding a huge and buoyant world market, transforming towns like Killybegs into areas of full employment and evident prosperity. But not every skipper around the coast was fishing by the rules, so all have been penalised with reduced EU quotas, and the penalties are being beefed up. Fishermen are up in arms, but all of us face national fines if they continue to transgress. Every TD with a constituency anywhere within an ass's roar of the sea has come under ferocious pressure from the fishermen to kill off or dilute the provisions of that Fisheries Bill, because not only are the penalties and forfeitures severe, infringements are criminal offences.

You see, fishermen might acknowledge that an odd rule might get broken and, while they know it's breaking the law, they don't see it as criminal activity. 'Anyway', they say, 'What about the Spanish, some of the French, too, those flags of convenience?'

In some Scandinavian waters, every fish caught must be landed and weighed. The general EU rule only weighs fish landed. So, thousands of tons of undersized fish are caught, killed and dumped back into the sea. They are not counted; they never existed. Stocks continue to decline. I followed in the wake of a small trawler in Dublin Bay across a carpet of tiny, dead, discarded plaice, boxes of them dumped to sort out maybe one or two boxes of commercially viable fish. Madness.

Inshore trawling is wiping out sea-angling tourism, which is worth more to the economy and impacts only a little on stocks. The new legislation is reluctant but inevitable. The rules are a mess, but without them neither fish nor fishermen have a future. But those rules must apply in and to every EU country.

Mr President

Broadcast 10 March 2006

One of many things that used to puzzle me as a young journalist was how the United States of America could hold in high regard presidents who were derided in Europe and revile men like Jimmy Carter who were well regarded outside the US. Bill Clinton managed to be well supported throughout most of his presidency on both sides of the Atlantic.

Ronald Reagan was depicted here as a bumbling fool, but I saw him work up close on the platform in Bally-poreen in 1984 when he very quickly realised that the carefully prepared script, the work of some zealous spin doctor, was a lemon. He quietly folded the cards carefully laid on the lectern and ad-libbed a real crowd-pleasing address. This was no fool. This was the poker player who broke the Soviet Union. America loved him, and no mud stuck to him. The Iran–Contra affair? Reagan remained pretty well unscathed.

I have just returned from a short holiday in America. First thing every morning and last thing every night, I scanned the news programmes. (It's a journalist thing; I really can't help myself.) Every morning, the hotel delivered a bulky daily newspaper, just in case I missed anything. And it's official: George Bush's popularity is at an all-time low. As ducks go, they don't get lamer! To understand why, you have to see things from a US point of view. The American president has two principal tasks. The secondary task is foreign policy; the primary one is to manage America. Hence, Jimmy Carter succeeded abroad and failed at home. Bill Clinton managed both with some success. George Bush is perceived as having some difficulty with foreign policy but has failed badly to manage America.

Hurricane Katrina may have blown herself out, but, months later, the storm over the Government's failures is still raging. New Orleans is in ruins. Only twenty of 120 schools are open. Most of its hospitals are still closed; indeed, most of its population still displaced. Canadian charity workers seem to be doing as much as anyone to help. There are accusations that George Bush's brother Jeb interceded to get a buddy who owns a cruise line the contract to house refugees from New Orleans, and now, before alternative housing is ready, those refugees are being turned out of the ships that want to go back to cruising.

Bush made security the mission of his presidency. Now, politicians across the spectrum are in furious revolt over his endorsement of a deal to sell America's principal seaports to an Arab-owned company. He has just concluded a deal with India, announced while I was in America, in which the US will provide nuclear technology to India. He sold the deal badly, telling the Indians, 'And we look forward to eating your mangos!' Mangos? For nuclear technology? Well, apart from the security considerations, America is in uproar over so many US manufacturing jobs going east, apparently with the support of their president.

The war in Iraq is going badly. The semi-professional National Guard units are suffering casualty rates of over

40 per cent. Americans love the military and support their soldiers, many of them kith and kin, but they are asking serious questions about their deployment by the administration. It's not hard to understand why. I saw scores of young GIs in their desert camouflage, the same age as my sons, polite young men and women, wandering around the duty-free in Shannon, using the phones there to call home. Some of them will not see their families again. It's easy to see why, for many Americans, the mistakes of the Administration are deeply personal.

Within six days of the first Normandy landings back in June 1944, General de Gaulle was in the town square in Bayeux reappointing the Civil Authority. As the Allies pushed forward, that Civil Authority was reappointed as quickly as possible. The periods of chaos were short. That was a largely American plan, but in Iraq the US Administration forgot all the lessons of the past and left their military in an appalling situation. For Americans, these are not anonymous soldiers, they're Joe the insurance salesman, Jimmy from the gas station, Pauline from the hairdresser's.

New Orleans or Iraq, Americans and their commentators seem to be concluding that this administration is good at making multi-billion-dollar deals but that the security and management of America are not in good hands.

We in Europe have much to thank the US for, including our freedom. Ireland survived for more than a century on money from America. America is well disposed towards Ireland. Don't forget the contribution to peace here made by the Clinton Administration and which continues, even if on a smaller scale, under Bush. Americans need our friendship, sympathy and support; that's what they have given us. George Bush is not America. Nearly two-thirds of Americans would like to see their president ride off into the sunset.

Growing pains

Broadcast 28 April 2006

I wonder if you have ever seen a television camera crew out covering a news story or making a documentary. The sound engineer frequently uses a directional microphone held just below the level of the lens so that it picks up the sound but it doesn't appear in the shot. The microphone is thus pointed upwards. Being sensitive, it is confounded by passing aircraft. Often enough, for example, I would be in full flow, burbling enthusiastically, when a pained look would seize the features of the sound engineer. He would take off his headphones and interject, 'No good; aircraft overhead.' And, sure enough, an aircraft would be passing over – not really intrusive to the human ear, but on a directional microphone enough to drown out my best efforts. Well, we would wait till Biggles had passed and start again.

In seventy-two episodes of *Out of the Blue*, it only became a serious problem when we filmed in Howth, in north County Dublin. It seemed that there was no more than a two-minute window of opportunity between passing aircraft going to or leaving Dublin Airport. Interviews had to be shot in short spasms, with lots of other pictures to cover the joins – a mere inconvenience to us.

That was a few years ago. Since then, flights have increased dramatically. Dublin Airport has got busier and busier. Roads around the airport are frequently choked.

The other day, it was reported in the *Irish Times* that 'Quick Park', the privately operated car park near the airport, had closed its advance bookings because of the volume of airport business. They have 3,500 parking spaces. The Airport Authority has 14,400 spaces in their long-term park and 3,600 in their short-term. The revenues are astronomical. The Dublin Airport Authority has an earning potential, from car parking, of 83,865,600 euro a year. It all adds up to congestion.

The infrastructure is under pressure, and that's before you get to the terminal building. Working flat out, its poor design can't cope comfortably with the numbers. Security has improved, and it is more efficient, but look around. There is no spare capacity. If you live on the flight paths, there is no respite. Planes land and take off at all hours. It's a miracle of air-traffic control.

There are some very good people working in aviation, make no mistake, but that airport is a national shame. The second terminal, not yet built, will have to be 50 per cent bigger than already planned. They're still building, trying to catch up, putting up a marquee this summer, we're told. (Dear Lord, please, not portable toilets.) Surely, all logic, forward thinking and good sense cries out for a second airport – one with space to grow, access and, dare I say it?, comfort.

No matter which way you look at it, Dublin Airport is bursting at the seams, and we are still looking at short-term solutions that aren't keeping pace with traffic volumes. Nearby Baldonnel aerodrome sits on a huge site, in an underpopulated area. It's the home of the Air Corps, the smallest branch of the Defence Forces. It's on a direct route from the south, close enough to shuttle for connections to Dublin Airport, almost infinite capacity for infrastructure – so, why not? It is owned, on our behalf, by the Department of Defence. That makes it easy for Government to make a decision.

London has, by my count, about five airports. Even Belfast has two. Airports attract investment, jobs and tourism. Air traffic has a heavy environmental footprint, but it seems fated to grow and grow. All our experience tells us that. Short-term solutions, 'make the books balance on my watch' management – well, that is called crisis management. Real management takes a long view, plans for the inevitable and engages in joined-up thinking.

Any of us who have had to use Dublin Airport marvel at how the staff cope with check-in desks which are located the wrong way around and much more. A 1960s airport still in the wrong century, this summer, will be airport purgatory. Dublin, a place where in July and August, 2 million souls will suffer for a while, but it will seem like eternity.

Gardaí in handcuffs

Broadcast 12 March 2006

According to An Taoiseach in the Dáil the other day, there are now 14,000 gardaí, with provision made for 3 million hours of garda overtime. The force now costs 1.3 billion euro per year. So why does it seem to us and to the Gardaí that there aren't enough of them? Maybe it's a question the newest recruit can answer. She is a top cop from Boston, familiar with a soaring murder rate and presumably well used to politicians demanding some good news for the electorate.

Over the past thirty years or so, most of the gardaí I have met have been decent solid types, shrewd and, yes, compassionate. They mostly act in a very considered way. All their training and experience teaches them to take a cool, appraising look. Of course, there are also bullies, head cases, time servers and wasters, much as you would find in any large organisation, but, in essence, like most of us, they are concerned with doing a job, raising a family, paying the mortgage; and, therefore, rogue gardaí make headlines because their conduct is so out of step with what we have come to expect from the force.

The Special Units have made armed robbery a much more precarious occupation. The National Drugs Unit can claim some considerable success. The Criminal Assets Bureau and all the other specialist units are undoubtedly needed. The Traffic Police have clearly a job to do.

The problem is that every time a special unit is formed, its members are drawn from the one pool of personnel, creating shortages in the areas of routine deployment, so anxious citizens no longer feel protected. Response times to minor crimes are poor. The force is stretched too thinly.

The rank-and-file gardaí are shouting this from the rooftops. The very senior gardaí don't complain publicly because every promotion above the rank of inspector is a cabinet appointment. Thus, an ambitious officer must be politically sensitive!

The great pity at the moment is that the Garda Representative Association has focused on the row over the garda reservists. There is a suspicion that they are trying to protect those 3 million hours of overtime and that the Department is simply trying to save money. Personally, I am in favour of a garda reserve, for lots of reasons, but the case for more full-timers also seems unanswerable.

And that raises questions about training and equipment. Only one garda in five is trained to use breath-testing equipment. One in five?! What do they actually do in Templemore? I bet they can all use a radar gun. Relatively few are trained as drivers, and the cars that they drive are often quite unsuitable for a modern force. Compare the vehicles to other European forces. Did you notice how few gardaí were fully equipped during the last Dublin riot?

There is now safety legislation on life jackets and behaviour afloat, but only a small unit of water-borne gardaí. In the garda stations around the coast, not even a pair of water wings and a set of flippers.

And then there is communications: it has taken four years to get the new phone system working. Even the

Taoiseach was scratching his head over that one! The resources were made available; the civil servants were tasked; and it has taken an incredible four years. For phones!

Modern police forces come equipped with lots of non-lethal weapons – ways of stopping but not killing: pepper sprays, baton rounds, tazers and so on – but it seems the choice for the garda is a baton or a gun. Remember Abbeylara.

The low level of physical equipment and training is nothing compared to the legislative tangle. The constraints on garda interrogations are loaded too heavily in favour of the suspect and, of course, thanks to abuses in places like Donegal, those constraints seem unlikely to be eased.

It is to the credit of the Gardaí that even in the face of such restrictions, they still manage to get convictions in some serious crimes. Organised crime in countries like America and Italy have needed special procedures and rules. Racketeering in the US is still a problem, but RICO laws (anti-racketeering legislation) have decimated organised crime.

Someone needs to come up with a practical shopping list because I believe that the politicians have the will to provide the cash. The rank and file are crying out. Public anxiety is increasing, so why is so little changing? Is the problem within the Department, or is it at senior garda level? That's the mystery, one that calls for some real detective work – maybe a job for a 'top cop' from the US!

In denial

Broadcast 12 March 2006

If you are an accident and emergency consultant who hasn't yet been interviewed on radio or television, don't worry: it seems that the story will run and run. Your turn will come. Keep the make-up kit handy; there is a camera crew coming your way soon! I don't know how Mary Harney or Brendan Drumm can be expected to sort out the advice, but at least there is no shortage of it. Oh yes – and here is some more.

Any good therapist will tell you that before you can be treated for a problem, you have to accept that you *have* a problem. You're not just a social drinker, you're an alcoholic. You're not just someone who dabbles in recreational drugs, you're an addict. So whenever a politician tells me, 'There is no crisis in the health service', I get quite depressed. Does that mean that the whole government is in denial, and, if so, how can the problem be treated? What comforts me is that the denial is a public, political denial and even the most detached citizen knows there is a crisis.

Politicians are not detached. They survive by keeping their fingers on their constituents' pulses. They know from the last batch of elections that health was the hottest item, and the Government got beaten up.[1] In about a

1 The European and local elections, 2004.

year, there will be a general election, just twelve months. Surely it's impossible to sort it all out in a year? Could there be substantial progress? A large number of step-down beds has been made available, but hospitals are still having to defer elective surgery because acute patients have to be treated first. Most agree that we need more beds, and with more beds comes the need for more personnel to tend to those beds; but additional beds won't be enough to relieve the chaos of A&E.

Part of the problem seems to be that in many hospitals, technicians work office hours. Expensive equipment, even X-ray, lies unused during the busiest times. That's not in every hospital, but it is in some. I recall waiting during an afternoon with a son who had broken a foot while the radiographer on duty was summoned by taxi to deal with the accumulated backlog. In short, it seemed good enough for the hospital that someone 'on duty' could stay at home until called on. Remember the name of that department, by the way: 'Accident and Emergency'.

Over the years, I have been fortunate in our choice of family doctor. I remember one night my mother was babysitting my then-three-year-old son. We came home to find the child struggling for breath and my mother trying to dial an ambulance. I called my doctor at 1 o'clock in the morning, and fifteen or twenty minutes later he was in the house holding the child over steaming pots of water. My son's breathing eased; possibly his life or his intellect were saved. Hilary was a great doctor, alas long dead, and with him any notion of calling a GP in an emergency.

We are all conditioned to head for A&E, but a HSE report showed that up to 50 per cent of those presenting at A&E had not been to their GP first, and a third of all of those turning up to A&E units could be treated by a properly equipped GP. Think about that. If, say, 300 people turned up at an A&E unit, 100 could have been treated elsewhere.

So why not? Opening hours are one reason; even large practices don't seem to offer twenty-four-hour cover, though proper shift arrangements could give both doctor and patient advantages.

There is no mandatory equipment level for a GP: hence, some practices are superbly geared up to conduct tests, do minor surgery and even offer a range of specialities; others have equipment levels that have changed little since the 1950s.

A few weeks ago, I was at the Irish Medical Organisation (IMO) Annual Conference where there were two interesting examples of denial: one from a junior minister, who, to the great amusement of many, announced that there was no crisis, and the other from the GPs, who insisted that they offered the optimum level of service. That's when up to 50 per cent of those taken ill headed for A&E and avoided them. And remember: a third of all A&E patients could be treated by those GPs. It was clear that some big practices in Cork were doing well with GP cover till 7pm and co-op cover after that, but nationwide, the GP service is uneven and placing an unfair burden on A&E.

Money plays a part. Why pay a GP to refer you to an A&E when you can cut out the middle man and go directly to hospital – pay only once. It might be worth considering deducting the GP fee, if paid, from the A&E charge, if levied, and allowing a practice to advertise its range of services and level of cover. Shock, horror! Actually stick a notice in the local paper and give GPs offering a good level of service equipment grants. Make it legal for GPs to have their own X-ray equipment – if the dentists can, why not the GPs? Take the handcuffs off the doctors and help them take one-third of patients out of the A&E units, and if they make more money by providing a better service, they will deserve it.

Oh, by the way, at that IMO conference, I heard the very persuasive Professor John Higgins, from Cork University Hospital, make the case for doctors to manage A&E and other services. Well, *Prime Time* pointed out that the most efficient of A&E units in the State is probably in Kilkenny, and it's run by a doctor. Not a computer expert or an accountant or a personnel officer: a doctor. Now there's a thing!

The law versus hormones

Broadcast 29 June 2006

Following the Supreme Court judgement that threw the laws on teen sex into disarray, what characterised events afterwards was haste. The public demanded that action be taken quickly, and it was, but that meant that thinking time was short.

Justice Adrian Hardiman's judgement that started the furore was a good one in law. For nearly every serious offence, guilt requires two essential ingredients: the intent and the act itself. Lawyers call these the *mens rea* and the *actus reus*. There are a few exceptions called 'absolute offences', mostly to do with motoring, where the prosecution has only to prove that the act occurred and the accused did it. Intent isn't relevant.

Hardiman correctly judged that where the accused can be deprived of their liberty for a very long time, the defence of having an honest belief that the sexual partner was over the legal age should be allowed to be pleaded.

There were what the Attorney General called 'communications issues' in his office, and a warning was not sounded that should the State lose the case, the legislation protecting young people would fall. Thus, there was no carefully thought-out statute waiting to be enacted. The situation was remedied in haste, and new laws were introduced. The age of consent was fixed at seventeen, subject to review. But the law is not gender-neutral. If two under-age people have sex, the girl commits no offence. The boy does. That could be unconstitutional – whatever its intention not to stigmatise under-age mothers. Pending a review, the Government wants to consult with teenagers. That, in brief, is the story so far.

What should be the legal situation? With the benefit of having had longer to think about it, a few things come to mind. It's a cop-out for parents to expect that a section of the penal code, in itself, can prevent teenagers having sex. Some years ago, friends of mine were trying to pick a secondary school for their two daughters and went to an open day in a very well-regarded school. They saw the labs and the sports facilities, heard about the academic achievements and the pupil–teacher ratio. Then came the pep talk from a famous teaching nun. 'We think', she said, 'that most girls will be drinking by the end of their second year. Most will be drinking vodka by the end of third year, and we don't think that there are many virgins in fourth year. You see, we can give your daughters a good education, but the rest is up to you.' My friends were shocked. How's that for a reality check? In essence, that means that it is up to parents to provide their children with as much information and guidance as they can. That's where the real protection lies.

There is a doctor I know whose daughters were sent to the teen disco with condoms – not as a licence but as a protection against disease and pregnancy, which that doctor saw in her surgery with alarming frequency. I was a little shocked when a friend in County Clare related her experiences running a teen disco. In the hormonal maelstrom, where there was no alcohol on the premises, those under-age teens were engaged in every kind of sexual activity.

Years ago, I agreed to pick up a son and his friends from a Junior Cert alcohol-free disco in a smart south Dublin hotel. Knowing the geography of the car park, I drove around the back of the building to park facing the exit. The headlights of the car illuminated a scene of debauchery: thirty or forty couples against a back wall. With some relief, I determined that none of the writhing bodies was a close relative.

No, it wasn't like that in my day, not at that age. Girls went out dancing wearing the Mary Quant panty-girdle, a double-gusseted affair made from trampoline-quality elastic, as impenetrable as any medieval contrivance. But the real inhibitor was fear.

We now live in an era where that fear has been removed. Legislation to protect teenagers from much older sexual predators is easy enough, but how do you protect them from each other? The hormones are raging. Youth is reckless, but do you really want to lock up a teenager for natural sexual activity? Because it *is* part of their nature. Do you think the law will inhibit them? Because I don't.

When our legislators were teenagers, pregnancy outside marriage was socially unacceptable. Little girls with child were packed off to hide their shame with relatives or in institutions. Thank God that that's changed. Condoms were unavailable; mortal sin was a cornerstone of belief. Waken up; it's all changed. You dress under-twelves like Britney Spears and then you are shocked when sex in adolescence becomes a rite of passage. Do you avoid embarrassing discussions at home and then become outraged that your children might be sexually active? Yes, the Government is right to consult with teenagers, lots of them, but it's not enough that they ask. Officialdom must, like parents, learn to listen. And, by the way, you won't like what you hear.

Shades of Grey

I've broadcast quite a few items about the elderly. The first time, in recent years, you heard an alarming discussion on the state of nursing homes and inspection procedures would have been on *Liveline*, which I was anchoring at the time. The discussion was depressing. If you are rapidly approaching old age, there is real terror that ill health will land you in a nursing home – but that's the *end* of the line.

To the young, old age begins while you are still in your fifties – still working, perhaps still supporting children through education. There comes a realisation that you are no longer an object of desire. For a man whose hairline is receding while his waistline is expanding, there is a slow dawning that he's not the man he used to be, physically. For a woman, the progress from young thing to 'oul one' can be very cruel because all of us, young and old, male and female, make superficial judgements.

To the hip-hop generation, we are the hip-op generation. It's not the fault of the young. We did the same. We eyed the jobs of older colleagues and sold ourselves as young, energetic, better. Society pursues the appearance of youth. Ageing is a genetic disorder we don't like to contemplate. We can retard the process, but only death can beat it. It's quite scary, and one of the ways we deal with fear is ridicule, so ageing and the aged become the butt of bad jokes and a process of disassociation. They become devalued and slip down society's priorities. As infirmity isolates the elderly, they vanish from sight, but long before that, they – we – have ceased to be valued. The clock is ticking.

Last in line

Broadcast 15 March 2005

It's nearly a year since, for the first time in a long time, the treatment of the elderly in care was given a public airing. It was RTÉ Radio 1's *Liveline* programme, and I was taking the calls that day. Now, of course, it is the focus of great media attention, which is concentrated on the illegal strip-mining of the assets of elderly people in nursing homes. Such attention is right and proper. Who knew about another missing file, a senior civil servant's word against the recollections of a former minister? The opposition parties looking for a scalp. Well, at least all of that concentrates the minds of civil servants, so-called special advisers and, of course, the ministers.

Two weeks ago, a retired public servant reminded me that not so long ago the person in care wasn't the only one whose means were tested before any subvention was paid. Their family was also means tested. That was changed, but the situation remained that the elderly person could only qualify for a full subvention when all that was left of their assets was the price of a modest funeral. I suppose the 'who knew what' debate is important, but it also served to distract from the quality of care. Caller after caller to *Liveline* told me about appalling conditions in some nursing homes. Some of those callers worked in those nursing homes. Inspection, it was alleged, was, at best, perfunctory and concentrated on checking the paperwork.

I know from personal experience that there are professional and compassionate staff and owners – great people. But from those phone calls, the worrying facts emerged that there are some very bad nursing homes, and there is no power to close them. In Scotland, a huge effort, I was told, is made to allow the elderly stay in their own homes: free installation of central heating, home helps, nursing visits, good GP back-up. The elderly prefer it, and it costs the State much less than residential care.

The UK has another very important provision, and I urge officialdom here to look at it. In the UK, the first three months of nursing-home care are free, regardless. That means if a stroke or accident victim makes a good recovery, they still have a home to which they can return. Here, the fees kick in from day one, and, frequently, even if there has been a good recovery, there is no home anymore, and the elderly person must end their days in care.

The elderly and their relatives here have the distinct impression that the system gives older people a very low priority. It has been said that the older you are, the further down the list you get for emergency care; that A&E units in some hospitals prioritise younger, fitter people. I've seen a woman in her late eighties with dementia, squirming in pain with a broken hip, sitting on a plastic chair for seven hours, incontinent, unfed, unmedicated, while young people with minor cuts and abrasions were treated. Eventually, the only people waiting in that unit were elderly. And then they were treated.

The State owes a duty of care to all its citizens, and a policy on the care and treatment of the elderly is urgently required, a written policy: clear and unambiguous. It was a campaign on *Live at Three* many, many years ago that raised the treatment of carers and got their meagre allowance paid directly to them. Why should it take media campaigns to change government policy? The elderly and their families are owed an awful lot more than a refund.

When care means more than
bed and board

Broadcast 7 June 2005

Excellent though the *Prime Time* television programme was,[1] it was by no means the first time I had heard all about nursing homes and their shortcomings. Indeed, I had listened to several days of discussion when I worked on *Liveline* last summer. Relatives called in with their experiences; nurses and other care workers came on the line; nursing-home operators joined in that discussion.

My own mother had spent the last two years of her life in a nursing home; and, as I listened to the many things wrong with so many nursing homes, I was grateful for the good fortune that had guided us to the place that would become her last home.

And then I realised that it wasn't entirely luck. My wife and a friend of hers, who lives in the area, toured various homes. I saw quite a few as well. One, for example, was simply too big, with scores of old people sitting on rows of seats staring into space, no stimulation. Others, quite clearly, had the *smell* of neglect. One was a beautiful place, very modern, very clean and absolutely *silent*. The residents spent most of their time in their own

1 On the Leas Cross nursing home.

rooms, alone. Not what I'd want. Eventually we visited one which was a large, old house, the kind of place that my mother would find familiar. You see, old people and ultra-modern don't necessarily go together.

As we arrived, unannounced, two elderly women and a care worker were having a cigarette in the porch. There was laughter and chat, humanity. The house was old but clean; it smelt right. Lunch was being cleared away; it looked good. The people who lived there were both public and private patients, and most, it would be fair to say, were confused but apparently content. We spent some time talking to the owner/manager, a well-qualified nurse in her own right. She told us about the block of new rooms being built onto the back. It seemed right, and my mother, although suffering from dementia, settled well and quickly. As the months went by, I became more convinced that we had actually found a very good home. It wasn't just hygiene and nourishment, it was seeing, for example, groups of elderly out in the garden in the summertime with ice-cream cones, hearing laughter.

My mother had always been an elegant woman, and when I called, unannounced, to take her out, she was smartly dressed, made up, hair groomed, which she couldn't do by herself any more. That was sensitivity, not show. It was respect for her. She was visited often, taken out for afternoon tea and a short drive, always happy to go back to her new home. Make no mistake, she needed an awful lot of care, with all the problems that come with dementia, but the mostly middle-aged women who worked shifts in the nursing home seemed to do that minding, not just with efficiency, but with compassion.

The first signs of neglect had nothing to do with the nursing home. They appeared when she was admitted to hospital after a fall and left unchanged to develop bedsores. An angry GP visited her and moved her to another hospital. The owner/manager of the nursing home also complained to that hospital and, indeed, helped nurse her back to physical health. The best care she received was in that nursing home; the very worst in a public bed in a large hospital.

Those *Liveline* callers repeatedly complained about inadequate inspection of nursing homes, but who is looking into the hospital care of the elderly, the attitude of public health to the elderly? The more I hear on radio and television, the more I appreciate the level of care that my mother had, which I believe she would have received even if she didn't have regular visits. But I do believe that the best form of inspection is unannounced visitation by relatives – ideally, forceful women who will look, check and raise Cain if it is wrong.

Most of those in nursing homes have had their assets, including their pension, stripped. They are entitled to keep their dignity. Don't lose sight of the fact that although there are many nursing homes that are truly appalling places, there are also good ones, owned and staffed by decent, caring people. The trick is to find them.

From what I have heard of inspection practices this side of the border, they are inadequate – advance warning and mostly a check of the paperwork, not the patients. So what's their best protection? Who is their best inspector? You are.

'Just a bit more than what you've got'

Broadcast 2 January 2006

Bear with me for a moment, because I have some regrets. The poet Thomas Hardy compared the ages of man to the times of the day in a poem called 'Eve', meaning evening. When I read it first at seventeen, it meant nothing. Forty years later, the last four lines have an alarming resonance: 'Time, to make me grieve, / Part steals, lets part abide; / And shakes this fragile frame at eve / With throbbings of noontide.'

Because, oh dear, yet another year has flashed past at warp speed; another digit has appeared on the odometer of life; one year closer to being completely clapped out. There are other alarming signs: the heavy stubble on the chins of my children (I have only sons, by the way); the failure to recognise new singing stars, to distinguish one from another; the increased amount of corduroy in my wardrobe; the high incidence of beige in my colour schemes – all sure signs of ageing. There is also a growing tendency to reminisce because events that to others seem like ancient history are still vivid for me, and I was reminded of one the other day.

Charlie McCreevy was hosting a lunch in Dublin during which he generously and jocularly referred to me as the man who first discovered him. The reference was to the election count in Kilkenny in 1979 during the European elections.

I recall a plump young fellow with a shaggy Beatle haircut and a brown pin-striped suit. He was leaning over the barrier behind which the boxes were being opened and sorted, the very early stages of the count. He was consulting a pile of school jotters covered in pencil notes and figures. 'What do you think?' was my idle enquiry. The answer was intriguing. His predictions, if true, would be disastrous for Fianna Fáil. All the more intriguing, since he turned out to be a young accountant elected for Fianna Fáil just two years earlier. He explained his predictions by referencing the pattern in boxes from the most remote parts of the constituency, faithfully recorded in those well-thumbed jotters.

Albert Reynolds was Director of Elections for Leinster, another new deputy, but already known as a skilled number cruncher. He was putting a brave face on it, and he dismissed those early predictions but appeared more and more concerned as he continued to make calculations on the back of a Benson & Hedges packet.

For want of something else to do, I filed young McCreevy's predictions to RTÉ in Dublin, complete with his extrapolations for the counts in the rest of the country. At first, they were dismissed; then it became clear that he had called it with 100-per-cent accuracy.

Well, McCreevy had become one of our star tallymen, and he spent subsequent elections as a studio analyst. His profile soared, but the key to McCreevy and his subsequent career, I suspect, came in the explanation he gave me in the wee small hours of the morning in Kilkenny all those years ago. 'The figures', he said, 'the figures don't lie, only the fellows who claim to know the figures lie.'

He is a trim, well-groomed EU commissioner now, with a retinue of staff and a fine wardrobe, but his strength, and some would say his weakness, is that twenty-seven years later, the figures for McCreevy still tell the story.

So, time and experience can provide an insight at times. Your own and other lives can be seen in a context, and you have enough material to bore for Ireland! Time teaches us lessons too: the pointlessness of vindictiveness, the futility of endless ambition.

As a youngster, I watched my hero, the dapper Alan Wicker interview Paul Getty, then the richest man in the world. 'How much money is enough, Mr Getty?' asked Wicker. The reptilian eyes narrowed, the mouth got even thinner, as Getty growled, 'Just a bit more than what you've got.' I wonder how many lives have been wasted trying to accumulate just a bit more when life itself is running out.

When ambition is sated and responsibilities largely discharged, there is a wonderful sense of liberation. I don't have to waste time doing things just to please others – being a courtier to the powerful who could advance my career or damage it. I don't go out of my way to be rude to people, but I am not the corporate creep I suspect I may once have been. I am not impressed by power. Those who have it only hold it in trust. They too will pass. And whilst I don't go around spluttering, 'I don't believe it', my tolerance for wasters has become a lot lower. Bad value, rotten service, poor manners are taken personally, not because I have been relieved of cash for something not worth it but because of the contempt, the disregard implicit in the fraud. I'm proud to be on the brink of curmudgeonhood where affectation gives way to practicality. Corduroy is warm and comfortable; beige is kind of cosy, gentle on the eye; but here's the best bit: if you don't like it, I don't care.

The twilight, not the shadows
Broadcast 20 February 2006

We make jokes about being old when we are merely growing old, and, indeed, for most people in their fifties, nightclubs, lots of late nights, the relentless energy of venues catering for much younger people have few attractions. We prefer a good dinner, a drink or two and a good night's sleep. There is a tacit acceptance that robust sports are not a great idea as we get older. We are more fragile, easier to break, slower to heal. Yet, we are merely getting older, not really aged.

We are still working, or just retired. There is still, in short, optimism. There remains the ability, energy and cash to make plans. There should be a period of liberation, when our children, if we have them, are independent, seen to and making their own way in life, perhaps now with children of their own. This golden period is dependent on a number of things: health, for example, sufficient income and the kind of support that we take for granted from family and friends.

A long time ago, the late Willie Bermingham, a Dublin fireman, called to a house in Clontarf to visit a retired journalist. That elderly journalist had been a well-known figure in his day but was now a widower on a pension. Willie told me that he found the man in a poor state, unable to look after himself, living in a big and valuable house with a fair pension, but quite alone. Willie told me he asked the man if he could do anything for him, and the reply was chilling: 'Just finish me off.' From that encounter, he founded the organisation called 'Alone' which sought to reach out to elderly people who had become isolated. There comes a point when old people become invisible. Out of sight is out of mind, and so, if an old person can't get out of the house easily, they become forgotten. Disability and death cull friends and contemporaries, partners and spouses.

There is an attitudinal problem in our society. The elderly are held in low esteem. They are more likely to need A&E services and end up in a hospital bed. Because the system has failed to provide recuperation beds, they get blamed for occupying critical-care beds. That's not fair. I have seen too the low priority given to the elderly in some A&E units. There are too few carers and beds and, it seems, no great will to change that system.

Mind you, it is too easy to blame the system. Advertisers, for example, have decreed the important target audience for programmers is aged between fifteen and thirty-five. These are the big spenders. The elderly are not considered important as an audience. They don't feature. They are invisible. Years ago, the elderly were integrated into the old local-authority areas. Close neighbours looked after the older ones. Children were brought up to run messages for those old neighbours, bring them cups of tea, look out for them. Their attitudes, by and large, were mindful and respectful. Now, housing policy creates special units for the elderly and little or no contact with other age groups. Youngsters develop negative attitudes to old people through media stereotyping and ill-judged jokes. The elderly are held in low esteem, and all the worse when their intellect begins to fail and confusion creates even greater anxiety. Dignity is lost with dependence.

I've seen those who care for the elderly with great dedication and compassion and humour, but it's too easy to see the old person in a single snapshot – now dependent, now needing care – and not the whole album of a life which, in many cases, did great things, raised a family, worked hard, kept the show on the road, earned their right to dignity and consideration.

I visited a relative in a nursing home last week. He suffered a stroke seven years ago, can't really communicate, seems to understand quite a bit, is confined to a wheelchair and has failing eyesight. He is very well minded by his family and by the staff. I know the man he was: a survivor of the North Atlantic convoys in the Second World War when seventeen out of every 100 merchant sailors died, a generous and humorous man, affectionate and honourable, now reduced by age and illness. He is not just an old man in a wheelchair; he is a person. So they all are.

When emigration saw the elderly left to cope on their own, there was, at least, the excuse of distance, but now the family is closer. To understand why one-off housing on paternal land is such a hot issue in rural Ireland, the urban dweller should know that it's more than economics. It's about the anxiety of growing old, alone and isolated, about the need to have family close.

To see more than a single snapshot would be a start. The onus is on us, who are merely getting older, to create a better life for those who are actually old, because it won't be long before we, too, are invisible.

The North and the South

Coming from Northern Ireland, I've seriously tried either to follow events there in hope or to banish them from my mind in despair. There is a huge period, perhaps twenty-five years, when no attempt at progress succeeded. The body count rose. People I know suffered. Some died. The North is a small place. Everyone I know there has been touched by the tragedy.

Many of my contemporaries did as I did and left. We made lives elsewhere in search of normality and security. We didn't want our children's identity defined by their religion. We didn't see a future for them or us in that dangerous place. But it stays in your soul. There is a frustration that so many good people won't see reason, that so much talent is wasted, lives disfigured.

At the time of writing, there is a new power-sharing executive in the North. Ian Paisley and Martin McGuinness are working together in government. I never thought I'd see the day. Tony Blair and Ian Paisley have paid glowing tribute to each other. Can it last? Dark forces may conspire with history to restore the chaos. Peace is fragile. Vigilance and goodwill are required.

The North is not, for many of us, a distant foreign place but somewhere close to our hearts as all of us struggle to escape from the poisonous quagmire of our history.

A new way of doing business

Broadcast 1 December 2003

The North's elections took up relatively little space in yesterday's Irish Sunday papers. The fine detail of election accountancy has been sorted out, who got what and what does it all mean. There are, especially south of the border, a number of, well, almost unspoken questions, such as 'Who gives a damn?', 'What's in it for us?' and 'Surely there is something better on the telly than this?'. I can understand that reaction. All of my life I have heard stalwart northern Calvinists talking about democracy, Britishness and the Union, whilst refusing to accept the majority who have voted to share power. They have been prepared to dress up in anoraks and march up and down with pickaxe handles in defiance of that crown to which they profess loyalty, even at one time, remember, flirting with a Rhodesian style UDI,[1] an illegal independence from the same much-loved crown.

At the core is a simple hatred of all things remotely Catholic. That's at the core. But the electorate are more sophisticated than you might think. Not every DUP voter is a rabid Catholic hater. And it would be a very serious mistake to think that any other than a relatively small group in the nationalist community would have voted

1 Unilateral Declaration of Independence.

Sinn Féin if a campaign of guerrilla warfare, the so-called armed struggle, was still happening.

The politicians have been analysing the messages sent by the voters – Sinn Féin, for example, unelectable in any significant numbers until they publicly renounced violence. The electorate have supported that renunciation. Of course, no dissident republican candidate appeared because amongst the nationalist community there is no appetite for violence. Don't think the IRA haven't got that message.

The unionist population is actually split three ways. There is the Trimble-led Unionist Party, prepared to share power but requiring more guarantees from armed republicanism. There is the Paisley-led DUP who won't, really, under any circumstances, share power with any Catholic, let alone an entire community.[1] But there is a third grouping. Let's call them pragmatic DUP. Peter Robinson, for example, might be edging in that direction. A substantial number of those who voted DUP did so knowing that at local-government level the DUP *does* business at the same table as Sinn Féin. There are people, of course, who abhor the thought that those whom they see as the same who murdered their kith and kin for thirty years should be rewarded with seats in government. And yet, those hard-headed Ulster Scots also know that there must be a way forward.

Maybe the Good Friday Agreement, however noble, was too much too soon for many unionists. The loud rhetoric screams 'No', but the phrase 'Not an inch' is not being proclaimed with any conviction. If Sinn Féin sits on

1 Never more delighted to be wrong. Other pundits beware: history can make a fool of you.

the policing boards, DUP man Sammy Wilson will stay on to protect the interests of the Protestant and unionist people. That's logical good sense, but it means sitting at the same table, and that's more than an inch: that's a *start*.

And what of the SDLP? Marginalised by London before the elections . . . was that a plan or a bungle? But I reckon that they are there for the long haul, so is the much-diminished Alliance Party, and don't be deceived by their abhorrence of violence, they are not lily-livered. Indeed, they have a toughness in the face of adversity that few others have. Like the official Unionist Party, there are no armed men behind them, no baseball bats, no pipe bombs or balaclavas, just a conviction that they are doing the right thing. These politicians are just as tough and resolute as any in Sinn Féin or the DUP.

On Friday morning, I heard that an Alliance man, Seamus Close, had been elected on the seventh count. Now, I haven't seen him for years, but nearly forty years ago we sat at adjacent desks at school. Ours was a kind of Tom-and-Jerry relationship: he would surreptitiously tie my shoelaces together; he was a small skinny fellow, and I would playfully hop him off a wall. He would come back laughing and easily effect an escape. We were, in fact, very, very good friends, but I always knew that of the two of us he was the tougher, and for thirty years he has fought an unpopular, and, to many, an unattractive, corner, under that moderate Alliance banner. Well, I reckon he is still as tough as ever, though I doubt that the Alliance Party has a terrific future.

One thing emerges from these elections, it is writ large: the gun is obsolete in northern politics. The electorate have made that clear. An overall majority want a power-sharing executive, but a majority of unionists aren't happy with the Good Friday Agreement, at least in its implementation. Be patient. This is a week for shouting, for celebration, triumphalism even and, of course, for recrimination. The real talking starts later. I'm not depressed. For thirty years, business as usual meant murder and mayhem. Talk? We can do that for a good while longer.

A quiet Friday afternoon

Broadcast 19 December 2003

I didn't actually hear the first bomb; that was on Parnell Street. I was still in the side-street cinema, having just watched the afternoon showing of the new Paul Newman/Robert Redford film, *The Sting*. I was working as RTÉ's night editor in a newsroom that then stopped transmitting at 11.45pm and didn't resume until 7 or 7.30 in the morning. I was also doing a few freelance bits and pieces for John Simpson, then the BBC correspondent in Dublin.

A quiet Friday afternoon, an opportunity not to be wasted. The movie ended. I walked the few yards back onto O'Connell Street, and then, from the street opposite, the boom and canyon echo of a bomb, a bloody bomb. Proof positive: the cloud of dust and birds that rose up into the early evening sky. I'd seen and heard that a score of times before in the North. In Dublin, crowds ran towards the blast. In the North, curiosity and compassion were tempered with caution.

No mobile phones then. I started running. Someone in Kap and Petersons near O'Connell Bridge let me use their phone. I called the RTÉ newsroom. I knew the numbers by heart but few of the journalists because of my solitary night shift. A reporter answered, and I told him that there were bombs going off in Dublin. He thanked me politely and hung up. He didn't ask for details, didn't route me through to a copy typist; in short, he didn't believe me. I phoned Simpson in the BBC office: he did believe me, and, by chance, a good freelance cameraman, Dave O'Connor from Bray, was with him.

South Leinster Street was devastated by the time we met at the bottom of Dawson Street. There were dazed and dying, dozens of helpers risking their own lives to help the wounded. There was carnage across Dublin. A well-known fashion photographer, I recall, was sobbing in a doorway, yet he went on to photograph the madness, as we did, before a BBC staff crew turned up. They had just arrived from London and were at once diverted to the bombings. Dave O'Connor and I were sent to Monaghan; seven dead there.

Now, the first question a journalist tries to answer is 'What happened?'. And that was painfully obvious, but it did take a lot of telling. The next question is, 'Who did it'? And, inextricably linked, 'Why?' Eoin Harris, writing in the *Sunday Independent*, made the point that events should be seen in context. He is right, of course; there is cause and effect. Things which don't excuse but do help to explain; for example, the arms-smuggling allegedly involving Irish cabinet ministers seems preposterous now but might well have seemed a good idea thirty-four years ago. You had to be there.

In 1974, the IRA had been bombing and shooting relentlessly. Amongst the loyalist paramilitaries, there was a lust for revenge. Pride needed a spectacular. And one of few questions answered definitively in the Barron Report was their capacity to build those bombs. The source of that conclusion is that popular oxymoron 'military intelligence'. But what was their source? How could they be so sure?

A lot of journalists were of the opinion that the loyalists had only one technician capable of constructing those devices at that particular time. His nickname was Tonto, but at that time he was known to be under lock and key in the North. I'd like some further proof that in May 1974 the UVF could make those devices unaided by any other group. Were they of similar design to other earlier bombs, for example, at Busáras, a bombing that stiffened the backbone of a government debating security legislation, an incident widely attributed to British agents? Did those bombs resemble the one detonated in the van carrying the Miami Showband? If so, there are other dark rumours that security-force handlers fixed that bomb to go off immediately, thereby ridding themselves of an unstable loyalist agent. The plan, the bombers thought, was to have the bomb go off a few miles down the road in the Republic.

The problems are huge. Inexperience, incompetence and a lack of cross-border cooperation means the forensic footprints are lost or blurred. It's also a grave error to expect that politicians given a brief in cabinet instantly become experts in that area. Generations of ministers have proven that fallacy.

In 1974, Patrick Cooney was Minister for Justice, a hard-line anti-subversive, a solicitor from Mullingar, punctiliously polite, dedicated to his brief, but with no special insights in how to deal with an atrocity like the Dublin and Monaghan bombings. The Barron Report accuses the Fine Gael–Labour coalition of not doing enough, of letting the files be closed after just twelve weeks. Could it have been that if a good case had been made for suggesting British security-force involvement, the effects on security here would have been devastating? Bloody Sunday in Derry caused a tidal wave of support for the IRA in the North. What effect a massacre in the South by even low-echelon RUC men or agents of the British Army, what effect would that have on security here if it could be proved?

There are questions that we are entitled to ask, and, as journalists, we are obliged to ask. When were the missing Department of Justice files last seen, and by whom? Did Jack Lynch's government ask to see them in 1977? His right-hand man then was Frank Dunlop. Yes, that Frank Dunlop.[1] Can he shed any light on them? Dessie O'Malley knows his way around the Department of Justice. What does he think? Surely someone in Charles Haughey's government would have wanted to review them? Garret FitzGerald's government? Who had them last? What long arm reached into that most secretive of departments and plucked out those files, and, above all, why? What's in those files?

Last week, there was great coverage in all of the papers, and then Saddam Hussein was found, and the Barron Report started to slip down the lists. It was a bit like that in 1974. It wasn't too long before other events displaced the Dublin and Monaghan bombings. More bombs, more carnage, more grief, more questions. Who set up the senior RUC men Harry Breen and Bob Buchanan? The lawyers Pat Finucane and Rosemary Nelson?

1 Star of recent corruption tribunals.

We have a good idea who pulled the triggers, but we need to know the hidden hands. Who advised and directed them? A tribunal and further Corry reports might provide some answers. I suspect the best we will get are a few more clues unless loyalists, republicans and the intelligence services come clean.

Dream on Derek, but keep asking the questions.

Speaking personally

Broadcast 23 December 2003

'Your thoughts, please, on the Northern Ireland elections', the producer asked, and I proudly completed the first draft that was as good a match for most of the essays about the North that you have heard, or read, for the last thirty years or so. They are largely the work of cerebral hacks who have hardly ventured a trembling toe north of the border. Oh, they may have talked to articulate paramilitaries, or former paramilitaries, but they have never seen their handiwork close up. Nor have they felt the pain and anger of people whose lives have been blighted by discrimination. You see, that's it, the intellectuals apply a scant knowledge to drive a certain logic without feeling anything, without knowing the coded phrases that reveal what's in the heart, a deep-burning hatred that defies logic, is almost impervious to reason but can, from time to time, yield to another instinct deep in the Ulster soul: common decency. None of the extreme elements trust each other, but perhaps a greater problem is the fact that too few moderate people trust those from the other community.

So, I'm speaking personally; very few journalists do that, and it may even be unprofessional. The first fifteen years of my career in journalism were spent in news and current affairs. They started in Belfast in the earliest days of the Troubles, but I was studying for A levels when

Peter Ward, a young barman, was shot down in Malvern Street and another young man was wounded. UVF man Gusty Spence and two other Neanderthals I can't recall were sentenced for that senseless and violent murder.

Ian Paisley had been in and out of the news during my growing up. His protest at a tricolour in the window of a Bord Fáilte office led to a riot and, of course, the headlines that that political pastor needed. But not since a lacklustre campaign in the 1950s had the IRA been active; no shootings, bombings, punishment beatings or racketeering. To all extents and purposes, the IRA was defunct. Nationalist representation in the Stormont Parliament was kept to a cleverly gerrymandered minimum.

The same rules applied to local authorities. Northern Ireland was a Protestant and, so far as it suited them, unionist fiefdom, but one always nervous of its southern neighbours and what it regarded as a fifth column of republicans lurking within the nationalist community. Lord Brookeborough, the long-serving Northern Ireland prime minister, set the tone by declaring that he would never employ a Catholic, and, if he did, he would have to sleep with a gun under his pillow. My slender, slightly built Church of Ireland grandfather faced down bully boys in the 1930s when they demanded that he sack his Catholic employees. He employed approximately 50 per cent Protestant and 50 per cent Catholic in the business, having the deep-seated conviction that it was the right thing to do. His son, my father, shared that conviction, but when he married my Roman Catholic mother, he had a grave concern that were I raised Catholic I would always be a second-class citizen in the Northern Ireland he knew.

As I reached my late teens, the young Austin Currie was prominent in highlighting the situation that led to the rallying cry, 'One man, one vote'. You see, unless you owned property or were a local-authority tenant, you didn't have a vote in local-authority elections. So, if a unionist-dominated council gave a Catholic, i.e., nationalist, family a house, they were also giving them a vote. Oh, and that wouldn't do at all, in their view. So in Dungannon, despite a housing list with many needy Catholic families on it, a single nineteen-year-old Protestant girl was allocated a house. The protests that followed may, in hindsight, have been the birth of the civil-rights movement. The UK Government really didn't want to know; decent unionists were uncomfortable but silent. The wretchedly neglected city of Derry was a pot on the boil.

Martin Luther King's example in America led to a peaceful and dignified protest, but the Minister for Home Affairs, William Craig, found his inspiration elsewhere, South Africa perhaps. It was Unionism's biggest mistake. The RUC, a paramilitary force by design, beat the protestors into the ground. The fuse was lit.

But know this, the IRA remained defunct. I remember the summer of 1969; it was savage. The Bogside in Derry was rioting, the Falls in Belfast came out too – until that night when a Protestant mob came over and started burning out Bombay Street. The people in the ghetto areas waited in vain for the trained and armed IRA battalions they had been assured *were* there for their protection. They were fictions of an eloquent bluffer.

I can tell you that the IRA presence that night amounted to no more than a handful of middle-aged republicans armed with relics from the 1950s or earlier. I know that because, unknowingly, I gave one of them a lift. I had been out with a girlfriend in Larne, saw the flames and tracer bullets light the sky on the way back to Belfast, so I drove a long loop around the city to get to her home over in the far reaches of the Upper Falls. Driving away, a bald bespectacled man I knew to be her neighbour flagged down my old Cortina and asked if I could get him down the road a bit. He had a canvas bag, and he was very agitated. He said people needed help, but he made very little sense. I assumed that he had medical supplies, but when I reached back to help him with the bag, I realised that there was a gun and ammunition in it. He grabbed the bag, and he ran off wheezing. That was an infamous night. Unionism was on the ropes, but the IRA's failure to protect would lead to a split, the formation of the Provisional IRA.

Constitutional politics was in trouble. The incompetence, not to mention the injustice, of internment gave the IRA a great boost.

I was a journalist, one who had seen our family business – we were art dealers – bomb-damaged five times. I was a journalist who had cleaned flesh blown from the bones of a neighbour from my shoes. I was a journalist who had seen the victims of bombing and torture too vile to recount. The sins of both sides. I left the North in fear and desperation, and I wasn't yet twenty-five.

I've visited often, but I've never lived there since. I remain fascinated by developments in the North. I watched it drop down the news lists; everyone was tired of it. But there was a tiny ember of hope left there, I couldn't see it at the time it was so faint. There was a number of unlikely people in an awful place at the right time. The persistent Hume; there was Adams and McGuinness; there was the extremely complex David Trimble, my childhood neighbour in Bangor; the loquacious David Irvine; the cold-eyed Billy Hutchinson; and others, of course. But it takes hard, tough, resolute people to make the peace and to keep selling it to others who are hurt, vengeful and distrustful and to some for whom peace means a loss of power, never mind a loss of income.

The northern elections will be noted by some people in other parts of this island; welcomed, perhaps, by some; ill-judged, mistimed might be the verdict of others. But, please accept this from me, someone who has seen the possible alternatives, the dead and the dying, the bereaved and the maimed. Any fair election in the North, free from fear and intimidation, is a triumph, almost regardless of the outcome. Democracy, wounded and weakened, is still alive. There is a strong pulse, and where there is that life, there is hope that common decency will triumph over hatred and distrust. That common sense will bring the gunmen out of the shadows to say truthfully, 'Look, there is nothing up my sleeve.'

Postscript

And there is, of course, a postscript to all of that.[1] That was then, this is now, well after the elections, elections that saw the DUP eclipse the Unionist Party led by David Trimble and Sinn Féin overtake the SDLP. Ian Paisley has emerged from a meeting in Downing Street to say the

1 Due to a huge public response, this column was re-broadcast with a postscript.

DUP will never share power with Sinn Féin. But then Peter Robinson hastened to pledge a constructive role. Jeffrey Donaldson has found a new home in the DUP. There is a lot more talking to do. The inquests are nearly over. The SDLP, marginalised by London before the elections, middle-aged in its membership and lacking John Hume's charisma, is taking stock. Sinn Féin knows that there is no political advantage in supporting gunplay. Another Canary Wharf can achieve nothing. They have their sights set on election south of the border. They must be unequivocally constitutional to build on their northern successes. The Ulster unionists remain, albeit diminished numerically, in support of power-sharing, but the DUP have a huge mandate built on unionist sensitivities and questions that must be addressed. It's all very difficult, very challenging, but it's all part of the democratic process.

To those who snort with frustration at the apparent impasse, I urge patience. Those with longer memories know a complex negotiation is infinitely preferable to bloodshed. No one in the world should take peace for granted. Be patient and just listen for a moment: this is yet another Christmas in Ireland when the guns are silent.

Irrational intolerance

Broadcast 31 January 2005

It wasn't the general message but the particular example of northern Protestant bigotry that caused such offence.[1] She hadn't included Catholics in her example. A hue and cry went up, and the President herself offered a fulsome apology, but her central message about irrational hatreds being passed on remains extremely relevant. Not every German was anti-Jewish, anti-Gypsy, anti-homosexual and anti-Slav, but very, very many accepted the propaganda because anti-Semitism, at least, was deeply rooted in the European psyche. It reached eager ears in England and in Ireland too. As millions died or were marked for death because of their Jewish bloodlines, an opposition deputy rose in Dáil Éireann to ask Mr de Valera, 'In view of the efficacious steps being taken by the German Government to deal with the Jewish problem, what steps are the Irish Government taking?' The man who posed that poisonous question served as a cabinet minister in the Labour–Fine Gael coalition between 1973 and 1977.

De Valera had a good relationship with the State's Jewish community but did little enough to offer sanctuary. Ireland was neutral, of course, but that neutrality was

1 In January 2005, President McAleese made a speech about bigotry and irrational hatred. She used by way of illustration Protestant bigotry in Northern Ireland.

very pro-Allied. Only a few hard-core IRA supported the German cause. One hundred and sixty-five thousand young Irishmen fought in the British Armed Forces. Flying boats were allowed to fly over Donegal to hunt U-boats. A Royal Naval vessel was based in Killybegs for the duration. British servicemen were whisked back over the border if they strayed into the Free State.

There were many other instances of pro-Allied behaviour, but very few of pro-Jewish activity. Immediately after the war, there was a prevailing sense of guilt: survivor's guilt that they had survived; Allied guilt that they had done so little. Even in Israel, the concentration-camp survivors were almost an embarrassment. Israeli leader, David Ben-Gurion called them scum. How did they survive? Why did so many walk to their deaths without a fight? It was the trial of Adolf Eichmann that let the survivors' voices be heard, and, at last, as the cruel efficiency of the Nazi killing lines was revealed, the survivors' stories came to light, and nations in denial finally started to face up to their shortcomings. But, of course, Ireland was neutral; we had nothing for which to apologise, no uncomfortable truth to face. By not acknowledging our sins of omission, we endorsed that anti-Semitism.

Irrational, racial or religious hatreds are often lethal. The differences between Belsen, Bosnia, Beirut or Belfast are ones of intensity, scale and efficiency. In the most devastatingly awful of these arenas, huge numbers were franchised by their leaders to hate and to kill.

That never happened in the North on that scale. Yes, there was, and maybe is, a genocidal gene in a far-out wing of loony loyalism – George Seawright, Johnny Adair, Lenny Murphy and others. Prejudice in the North most frequently showed itself in discrimination which could have led to widespread ethnic cleansing, and there was some, but not slaughter on a scale other parts of the world have seen. The late Cardinal Ó Fiaich said that 'Protestant bigotry was based on religion, Catholic bigotry on politics.' True enough, perhaps, at the time, but it was still bigotry, and, indeed, some Catholic bigotry was rooted in religion.

Those in denial of bigotry should have listened to the blood-and-thunder speeches at the field on the Twelfth of July. Not the slightly toned-down ones of the past decade or so; but I heard, growing up in the North, strange things. No nationalist politician ever spoke like that. Many Protestants found that kind of Twelfth of July rhetoric either embarrassing or just so much harmless hokum.

I grew up in a Protestant town, a good town, with mostly Protestant friends. I went to a Protestant preparatory school; indeed, I had a Protestant father. And, though people of that class rarely joined the Orange Order, there was a tacit acceptance that Catholics were, in some way, second class. That was an attitude undoubtedly handed down; perhaps it still is. Neither community entirely trusts or understands the other, though be in no doubt there is great decency and goodwill on both sides now. But each must look to their conscience – the churches, for example. Early in my teens, the liturgy contained the phrase, 'The perfidious Jew'. An embarrassing line, now deleted. Words can be very dangerous. The Orange Order cancelled its meeting with Mary McAleese because of her ill-chosen words. Did they see the mote in her eye but not the beam in their own? Have their words all this time been so well chosen?

Mary McAleese has apologised, but there are others who should also examine their words, and not just the carefully cloaked public ones but the poisonous remarks made in private, about those of different race, colour, religion or politics, words that fall on young ears. You see, Mary McAleese is right: intolerance is an inherited disease.

A brutal and hysterical cycle

Broadcast 16 September 2005

It's depressing to see disturbances in Belfast again, and those concerned observers are asking intelligent and reasonable questions: 'Why?' 'What has driven the loyalists of Belfast to take to the streets and even open fire on crown forces?' The problem is that, by the standards of recent debate, the answers are neither reasonable nor intelligent. It's part of a brutal and hysterical cycle that may have started in 1822. That's the date, some say, when Belfast saw its very first sectarian riot. It was apparently fomented by a hell-fire Calvinist preacher, the Revd Henry Cooke. He delivered his anti-papist message on the steps of the Customs House. From then on, at very regular intervals, there were riots and often deaths. An Anglican wit, visiting Belfast in the nineteenth century and witnessing one such riot where the rocks flew, observed, 'I have often pondered the connection here between theology and geology.'

Recently, the *Irish Independent* published extracts from the paper over a century or so of news coverage, and quite regularly there had been reports of fatalities arising from riots in Belfast. They are nothing new. But why would so-called loyalists take on the forces of the Crown? That too, of course, is nothing new. When push comes to shove, loyal Ulster will mobilise in defiance of the very crown to which it swears allegiance.

When the Home Rule Bill was being discussed in the 1900s, thousands of men signed an oath in blood. In 1912, a huge consignment of German guns came into Larne on board a ship called the *Clyde Valley*. And what was the rallying cry of Protestant Ulster? 'Home Rule is Rome Rule.' Stamped on the gun butts was the slogan, 'For God and Ulster.' This unofficial army was the Ulster Volunteer Force, the UVF, but every speech, every motto, had a religious reference or resonance.

The learned analysts rightly point at the modern UVF and their attempts to distract police from investigating their murderous feud with the breakaway LVF.[1] They explain the involvement of that organisation. The UVF had, only a short time earlier, organised very similar street disturbances during searches by the Police for arms. The UVF had its own agenda, but it was happy to provide the muscle for the Orange Order, who were protesting – wait for it – at not having the right to march triumphantly and in large numbers through a predominantly Catholic area. Why would they want to? And who are they? They are men who feel the need to prove that they can still keep the Taigs in their place, can still let West Belfast hear the war drums.

There are two principal Orange populations, one urban, one rural; the difference is that nearly all the Orangemen in the city are working-class Protestants, while rural Ulster offers more of a mix economically and educationally. To this day, almost every aspiring unionist politician feels the need to join an Orange lodge.

1 Loyalist Volunteer Force.

Middle-class unionists realise this. I know that it's just something their politicians have to do. David Trimble is a member, but the Order still withdrew its support when he stood by the Good Friday Agreement, or at least a fair bit of it. Apologists for Orangeism say it stands for religious tolerance for all, and there are some learned book writers who clearly believe them, but they can't have listened to the rhetoric. They must have overlooked the expulsion of those who attended a Roman Catholic church service. Wedding? Funeral? Go to that, and you're out, brother.

No organisation embodies religious bigotry in the North more than the Orange Order. The UDA is an avowedly, anti-nationalist organisation, but it's really about drug-dealing and extortion, bling, fast cars, murder for territorial control and the right to sell drugs. The UVF is embroiled in internecine feuding, though its members still kill the odd Catholic for sport. The one organisation that still has religious difference as its *raison d'être* is the Orange Order. I served Orangemen in the bar where I worked as a schoolboy. The Orange Hall was on the other side of the street. The local men were decent enough, but the Glasgow bands they hired for the Twelfth were scary, vicious and threatening. It was the 1960s. The Catholics knew their place; the pot hadn't boiled over.

My Church of Ireland father was married to my Roman Catholic mother. My father was a big former rugby player, dark complexioned and mercurial of temperament; it was a brave and foolish man who insulted his wife. Fifty per cent of his workforce was Catholic, a policy his father had adopted. They had something else in common: they despised the Orange Order. My father's life in Belfast had been interrupted at regular intervals by sectarian riots. He couldn't understand the gullibility of those prepared to go out and riot, their readiness to swallow any improbable lie, to bully and to intimidate. The Order's weasel words, 'blaming the Police', fooled only those who wanted to be fooled. The pictures are there: Orangemen hurling rocks, wielding swords, at one with the massed youths, destroying their own areas, apparently unperturbed by the 150 or so live rounds fired by paramilitary gunmen in their name. One unionist friend of mine I was due to visit this week advised against it. He said, with no conscious irony, 'You know, they're worse than republicans.'

In the interest of mutual respect, we all go easy on the Orange Order yet ignore the plight of working-class Protestant Belfast, ill served by cowardly and ineffectual politicians, afraid to criticise the paramilitary gangsters, without meaningful investment because no business wants to pay protection money (Why set up in an area controlled by hoods?), without jobs because the traditional Protestant jobs in the likes of Harland and Wolff no longer exist? Traditional apprenticeships are very few. Hope is in short supply. Protestant working-class Belfast has, as ever, been diverted from the real issues by the Orange Order.

Groaning with guns

Broadcast 27 September 2005

If the guns of the Provisional IRA have really been put away for good, it should be a source of great rejoicing, but it is appropriate to think of the horrors that those guns have perpetrated: the thousands dead, injured and bereaved – cold comfort for them. Good men, men of faith and integrity, have vouched for the decommissioning of guns and explosives, so we hope that what we learn from them is the whole truth.

The North was groaning with guns for all of my life. The visible ones were in the hands of the security forces, including the infamous B-Special Constabulary, whose membership standards were appallingly low. There was a lacklustre IRA campaign in the 1950s, which effectively ended when Seán South was shot in the back of a lorry trying to raid for guns. Interestingly, one of those who took part in the campaign was the politician Paddy Devlin, and it is also worth noting that years later he was a fervent democrat, who dedicated himself to the peaceful pursuit of justice, at considerable personal risk.

One of the great strokes of the British Army was the disarming of the B-Specials. They asked them to report to barracks with their arms, and, as each arrived, they were disarmed and then disbanded – those guns effectively decommissioned.

Before that, I remember August 1969, when B-Special armoured cars straffed houses in the Lower Falls with .5-calibre Browning machine guns, a ten-year-old boy called Rooney shot dead on the floor of his bedroom. I recall the empty IRA promises of men and arms ready to defend the Catholic areas, the unbelievable story that the IRA had sold its ageing arsenal to the Free Wales Army, and the hard men from the Falls and the Ardoyne and other areas splitting away to form the Provisional IRA and the start of an armed campaign that would blight three decades.

Dundalk had so many fugitive gunmen it was nick-named 'El Paso'. Still, because injustice persisted, there was ambivalence. It is to the great credit of Paddy Devlin, Gerry Fitt, John Hume, Paddy O'Hanlon and many others that they stuck to their moral guns and did not turn in any way to the kind of guns that kill.

By the mid-1970s, the old Stormont Government had gone, there were sweeping reforms in housing, but attitudes had hardened, especially after Bloody Sunday. The issues that brought thousands of civil-rights marchers out onto the streets – many of them young Protestants, by the way – had been resolved. Gerry Fitt's role in that has been overlooked. He was the man who had brought British parliamentarians to the North, who, with his colleagues and what would become the SDLP, achieved through politics what the gun had failed to get in successive IRA campaigns. All that done, thirty years ago. The only remaining aim for the disaffected was a thirty-two-county united Ireland, physical borders disappeared with a common market. What was left? Revenge? Power? An investment in guns, lives, jail time that made not one whit of democratic progress or reconciliation.

I know families in the North whose children gave their lives, or took the lives of others, to achieve nothing. Tragedies. I have contemporaries of school and university who took up the gun. They weren't monsters. They were good-humoured, generous and wrong. A few are dead; in fact, most of that generation. They're forgotten now, except by their families and friends. A blood sacrifice on an altar already soaked.

The gun had brought Irish unity? No. Not one inch closer – and what do we mean by unity anyway? Geographical lines on a road? A population joining a common cause in a spirit of brotherhood? Well, you can't point a gun at someone and convince them of your good faith. You can't blow them up and win their confidence. Paddy Devlin knew – and he had suffered at the hands of the Provisional IRA as well as loyalists – that the gun and the bomb didn't work. My heroes had no armies behind them.

There's a problem with guns, and we've seen it in the gangster wars here in the South of Ireland, the murder rate in the US too, and in other places where guns are easily available. As a dispute escalates, it's just too easy to reach for a gun to settle things once and for all, except that it rarely does. Blood calls for blood. In short, if someone owns a gun, designed to kill people, sooner or later someone gets killed. So, rejoice if hundreds – who knows, maybe thousands – of them have been decommissioned.

Guns aren't the only things that kill. Robert McCartney, for example, was knifed to death. It's not enough to decommission the guns or even 'not to condone' a killing. There must be law, supported by a community and their leaders. Ordinary people mustn't swap the tyranny of 1960s unionism for that of modern paramilitarism, and yet, throughout the North, this is so often the case.

So, will there be progress? Decommissioning is a huge step, and it's more than symbolic. The DUP protest that it's not transparent enough. Ian Paisley's photo album is missing its trophy shots. But for what it's worth, I believe, that except for bits and scraps, the IRA arsenal is gone. It's not possible to account for every bullet, and if the reports of the monitoring body over the next months give Sinn Féin a clean bill of health, the DUP will come under increasing pressure to enter talks with Sinn Féin. A taste of peace, we hope.

Decommissioning the guns and explosives is a huge step. But decommissioning hatred, distrust and prejudice, that's going to be much, much harder. People also need to know the truth. Who killed whom? Where are the bodies? Who colluded in killings? Why were certain investigations not pursued? Unfortunately, the truth was decommissioned years ago.

Spies and Stormontgate

Broadcast 16 January 2006

Ah, the good old days. The phrase, of course, means different things to different people. To old journalists, it
recalls a time when you could see and believe the hand
of intelligence agencies at almost every twist and turn of
events in the North. We knew who the CIA Resident in
Dublin was; we were meant to, of course, because I suspect the real CIA information-gathering operation was
probably run by deep-cover agents who didn't even
enjoy diplomatic status.

I came across one in the early 1970s, posing as a journalist working for an American company, a subsidiary of a
major network specialising in serving small radio stations
with a syndicated news service. The cover, of course, was
perfect: low profile, a genuine news service, a reason to be
in trouble spots, an excuse for talking to paramilitaries and
other players in the unfolding drama. He blew his cover
when a loyalist bomb went off in a republican area and he
took a lift to the scene with a young Protestant civilian who
was just curious and perhaps flattered by the friendship of
an American newsman. They were grabbed by local republicans: the American was released; the young man with him
was murdered. By the end of the day, the American was on
a plane out, and next morning two RUC Special Branch
detectives paid his bill at the Europa Hotel. QED for most of
the bona-fide journalists at the time.

British Intelligence seemed to be just as obvious at first. The RUC Special Branch undoubtedly had the best network of informers and, indeed, probably the most accurate information, but there were early rivalries between them and Military Intelligence, that famous oxymoron.

The British Army Press Officer in Lisburn was a man called Captain Colin Wallace, who sounded upper-crust and, indeed, appeared to be an old Etonion but was actually from Ballymoney. His title 'Press Officer' but his true vocation 'black propaganda'. He resigned to become Army PRO for Ian Smith's Rhodesian regime. When that job ended, he returned to England and was convicted of murdering his girlfriend's husband with a karate chop and of dumping his body in the river. He won his freedom by claiming that he was framed by British Intelligence to keep him quiet. He cast sufficient doubt on the conviction to have it set aside. Then he made a number of astounding revelations, or claims, that elements in the intelligence community had plotted against British Prime Minister Harold Wilson. A Captain Holroyd made other claims about black operations in the North.

Of course, by then, the hands of the intelligence services were seen everywhere – and there lay a problem. There were too many of them, competing, often against each other. So Mrs Thatcher sent in Sir Maurice Oldfield as Security Coordinator. He brought in a team of senior intelligence mandarins. Oldfield, it is said, was the character on which John le Carré based his spymaster, George Smiley.

It's probably no coincidence that from then on the development of agents within every faction on the island was given priority. Those deep in the IRA seem to have provided information, some of which undoubtedly thwarted IRA operations and almost certainly led to the arrest or deaths of IRA men. Loyalist agents were active in assassinations. It was, and is, a murky business, where the only morality is that the end justifies the means. It was clear that at least some operatives were out of control: judge, jury and, at least by proxy, executioner.

No journalist can even guess now the level of penetration of Sinn Féin, a primary target, or of the loyalist paramilitaries, the political parties, the Gardaí perhaps. The British certainly had an agent there back in the 1970s. The acquisition of intelligence information can, of course, save lives. Did the agent Kevin Fulton really try to tip off the Gardaí about the Omagh bomb? Someone has clearly thwarted further bombing attempts by dissident republican groups.

But Stormontgate is something else. Did British intelligence, or elements therein, somehow deliberately engineer the downfall of the power-sharing administration in the North? When Mr Donaldson made his statement to RTÉ admitting his role as a British agent, he added that he had had no contact with his British handlers for several years.[1] Does that mean that the British have another well-placed agent, the one who told them about, or who engineered, the Sinn Féin spying operation? Well, we don't even know who to ask any more.

Ah, the good old days, when a properly accredited journalist could have a gin and tonic with a bloke whose

1 A short time later, Denis Donaldson was found murdered in a cottage in Donegal.

stiff upper lip and posh accent screamed honesty and integrity, when we knew not to believe a word he said and were reassured that he was really too busy plotting against his own prime minister and wrong-footing the real enemies, members of the other branches of the security services. Oh yes, those were the days.

Bringing it to the boil

Broadcast 10 February 2006

Everyone gets angry from time to time. Anger is a normal human emotion – someone cuts you up in traffic, you get angry. It becomes unacceptable when you succumb to rage and react in a way that is disproportionate: getting violent, for example, reaching for an axe. There is, if you like, a spectrum of dissatisfaction that starts with annoyance and heats up all the way to blind fury. I get annoyed when politicians, policemen and other journalists blindly buy into the fiction that speed, per se, is the primary cause of serious accidents when the official analysis shows that 88 per cent of such accidents are caused by bad driving, of which speed is only one possible component. I get annoyed, but I don't rush out and burn a garda station! Is that because I'm civilised or just not angry enough?

People in Ireland are shocked at the reaction of the Muslim world to cartoons in a Danish publication that lampooned the Prophet Mohammed. We are shocked because we don't share the same terms of reference, can't understand the depth of feeling, the hurt and the anger. And we should make an effort to comprehend. Even if we can't grasp the reasons for the intensity of Muslim anger, we do know a bit about riots.

The first one I saw was about forty years ago in Belfast, without a Muslim in sight, I might add. An Irish tricolour was displayed in the window of what I think was a Bord Fáilte office. The Revd Ian Paisley led a protest. There was, of course, a counter-demonstration, and a riot ensued. Middle-class Northern Ireland really didn't give two hoots, but to hot Orange Belfast, that tricolour was more provocative than pictures of King Billy in a frock. The riot achieved little except to raise the profile of Ian Paisley. He was the man who told loyalists that they should be offended, the depth of the offence and that it was their duty to protest.

That's something else I have learned about riots: they have to be organised. A mob needs to be franchised by inflammatory speeches or a group who have turned up equipped to burn. A group of Muslims apparently toured the Middle East with copies of the Danish cartoons and also, it is reported, with others which weren't printed at all! These were unspeakably offensive, depicting the prophet as a paedophile, a consumer of alcohol and worse. This means that a deliberate attempt was made to crank up the anger, to manipulate the faithful. And that's another thing about riots: they are, maybe, sparked off by a specific incident, but they won't happen without some deep underlying reason.

Don't feel too superior. I've watched many riots in the North arising from specific incidents of territorial encroachment by one group onto another's patch. Parades are always a great excuse, but the underlying causes were hatred and distrust, bred by that most accursed of things, history.

Maybe you are too young or too forgetful to recall that in the early 1970s the British Embassy in Dublin was burned. No, no, not a Muslim to be seen. That riot was inspired by the Bloody Sunday killings four days before. A protest became a riot; some had clearly come equipped; the embassy burned. This island has seen lots of riots, and they have all had a few essential ingredients: a trigger or incident, a focus, an underlying hatred and the will by a few to lead the many, to up the ante and exploit the emotions of the crowd for their own aims.

What's happened in the past week in the Middle East has a familiar ring: the trigger, of course, the publication of those Danish cartoons that many Muslims found profoundly offensive. There was also a concerted effort by others to rush around the world, to make sure as many as possible were offended. At least two national governments, Iran and Syria, seem to have helped orchestrate these protests for their own purposes. Without a deep underlying hatred and distrust, all this would have little significance. The West, and that includes us, needs to address this. It's not a question of appeasing. It's about understanding and, in so doing, not causing profound offence and hurt unintentionally, not providing those whose intentions are sinister with a means of fomenting more hatred. Free speech, sure – but you know, everyone has a boiling point. Who knows, if you said certain things to me, the most reasonable of men, in my own judgement, you might get a punch in the nose.

Anatomy of a riot

Broadcast 17 February 2006

Some of you will recall, I've spoken about the anatomy of a riot. Such events seldom, if ever, happen spontaneously; they require a number of essential ingredients. Recent events in Dublin were a classic example.

The recipe is as follows: a cause that can be used to outrage those disposed to be outraged or provide an excuse for those who want to vent their spleen. Territorial encroachments on this island are a standard excuse. So you have got Orange bands proposing to march in Dublin, a Heaven-sent opportunity for this republic to show its devotion to true republican ideals and tolerate a protest by those with whom we disagree but who nonetheless have a right to peaceful protest; also, sadly, an excuse for those who merely use the republican label as an excuse for evil, for sectarianism, who metaphorically and literally wrap the green flag around them – without seeing it, because the colours of that flag are symbolic: the green for nationalism, the orange for unionism and the white for peace and tolerance. The only flag those who rioted should have waved would have been bitter lemon.

The next ingredient is motivation by way of rabble-rousing and organisation. Within a short period of time, the Taoiseach was able to refer to stashes of bottles left in laneways the night before. Reports refer to petrol bombs. No one brings a petrol bomb to a peaceful protest. And when all the ingredients are in place and you have means and motive, there remains only opportunity. Add that, and you have your riot, with all its potential for death and destruction.

It's under that last heading, 'opportunity', that you must question the actions of the authorities. The gardaí on duty acted with the utmost valour, and quite a few ended up in hospital. My colleague, Charlie Bird, was saved from serious injury by two plain-clothes men who waded in. Clearly though, there were too few gardaí with not enough equipment and, to any experienced riot-watcher, poorly deployed.

Perhaps because of the fallout from the 'Reclaim the Streets' protests, there seemed to be a reluctance to draw and use batons, the only weapon the Gardaí have. No water cannon or any other riot weapon. No closing off of laneways and side streets. No well-trained snatch squads. Just a few valiant gardaí stood between us and anarchy. They deserve better.

There was an admitted failure of intelligence, which leads me to doubt if Sinn Féin were centrally involved, because they are riddled with informants, and they've nothing to gain. But early in the morning, did no one check for bottles, or worse, stashed in the area? Were there no perimeter checks by garda observers keeping an eye on those coming into the area? Was the possibility of a full-scale riot not even contemplated? Are speed cameras the only bit of modern equipment the force owns?

I know a few gardaí, and there *is* anger. At least one blamed the accountancy mentality that measures the cost of garda overtime and deployment against the chances of a full-scale riot. A calculation that was wrong and that put garda and civilian lives in danger. And one thing is certain: if that calculation was made, those who made it weren't shoulder to shoulder with their hard-pressed subordinates on O'Connell Street. If the gardaí on duty were overwhelmed, was there a contingency plan, a unit of properly trained army on standby? More gardaí tucked away somewhere? I suspect not. That's very dangerous. The people who organised that riot now know just how close they came to taking control of the centre of the capital, and they will have another go in the full knowledge now of what it will take. Given the means and the motive, they will seize the opportunity.

It was useful for the rioters that a helpful local authority had left, in Brian Dobson's words, 'an ammunition dump' in the middle of O'Connell Street – all that building material poorly protected. A pilferer might be deterred, but a rioting mob? Would the PSNI[1] have allowed that? Why would our security forces not insist that all that potential ammunition be decommissioned? To the unionists and hard-line loyalists went a huge propaganda victory. According to one commentator, the definitive end of the peace process. To the rioters: revenge, elation perhaps at getting away with it, the booty from looting, the bully strut, the unholy glee from causing destruction and injury. To the rest of us: anger, shame and the need for answers from those whom we elect or appoint to protect us and our society. We need accountability for those salaries paid and that performance *not* delivered.

1 The Police Service of Northern Ireland.

That would be an ecumenical matter

Broadcast 21 April 2006

Who would have imagined that the most controversial part of the 1916 commemorations would be a concele-brated mass. It took place on Easter Sunday at the Augustinian Priory in Drogheda. The mass also remembered those who fell at the First World War Battle of the Somme. The mass was organised by Fr. Iggy O'Donovan, and he invited the local Church of Ireland rector, the Revd Michael Graham.

In a slow week for news, it has been a godsend for the media. Once again, my colleagues have grappled with theology, because the Primates are not pleased. The Church of Ireland Primate, the Most Revd Robin Eames is quoted as saying, 'Such occasions, while well intentioned, can lead to misunderstandings and misinterpretations.' The Roman Catholic Primate, Archbishop Sean Brady said, 'There was a real danger of causing widespread confusion, raising false hopes and creating situations that are open to misunderstandings and manipulation.'

Of course, by now you will have heard all of that. I wonder if you are as confused as I am? You see, I was brought up as a Roman Catholic because of the traditional prenuptial agreement between partners in a mixed marriage. Although I went to a predominantly Protestant preparatory school, I was excused Protestant bible studies and sent over to the local Convent of Mercy every Saturday morning for two hours of religious instruction from Mother Paul, a bright and charming woman who would swat any really difficult questions with a stock answer, 'Ah, that would be a question for a theologian.'

At Roman Catholic secondary schools, I was the precocious star of the religious-education classes. I suppose, on reflection, I was trying to find out what were the apparently enormous differences between the faiths of my Roman Catholic mother and my Church of Ireland father and why would these broadly delineate the politics of their adherence. The theological differences are easy enough to note: the authority of Rome, the interpretation of the Eucharist and the doctrine of transubstantiation and, well, that's really just about it. Female clergy? Married clergy? Birth control? Well that's about the authority of Rome.

Rome even accepts, I believe, the validity of Anglican ordination. The differences between the two churches seem to me small compared with what they had in common: the worship of the same Christian God, the adherence to the same set of commandments, the same hierarchical structures, very similar services too. Surely there can be no good reason why the two churches could not just worship together but even celebrate the same religious services? Transubstantiation is in the heart of the believer.

Greater by far are the political differences, spawned by history and fostered by the imperial power.

There is always a problem trying to understand an event like the 1916 uprising and episodes during it without seeing the broader historical context. For example, we are told the Volunteers knelt to say the rosary, but it seems they were sending out a message to the Roman Catholic hierarchy who had condemned the Fenians fifty years earlier and which condemnation had undermined support for the Fenian cause. This time, many senior members of the hierarchy were, at the very least, reluctant to condemn.

To understand the continuance of religious political splitting, you have to go back to 1798 and the United Irishmen. It suited both the northern unionist and the Irish governments to airbrush the northern United Irishmen out of history – because in the North that rebellion was largely Protestant. Kelly from Killane and Fr. Murphy are celebrated here, but how many songs have you heard about Henry Joy McCracken? How often is his execution in Belfast's Cornmarket recalled? How many know that Lord Castlereagh apparently cut McCracken's throat on the gallows? That Roddy McCorley was a Protestant farmboy, hunted down and hanged a year after the uprising was crushed, or the nameless Presbyterian ministers skinned alive or hanged from the gable walls of their little churches? That was a noble uprising, and their memories deserve better, but then, they were Protestants.

The imperial power fostered religious differences as a way of dividing and controlling Ireland. The Orange Order would be nurtured. In Belfast, the Revd Henry Cooke, and, later, 'Roaring' Hugh Hanna would help foment sectarian tension. There had always been friction between the Planter and the Gael. Despite the high profile of patriotic Protestants like Wolfe Tone – and, later on, men like Douglas Hyde – it suited both politicians and prelates to emphasise the differences between the churches rather than that which united them.

I know that both primates are keen, if cautious, ecumenists, both reluctant prisoners of centuries of difference. But, in this instance, Fr. Iggy O'Donovan, I believe, has correctly identified an important symbolic act of religious and perhaps political unity in putting aside differences to join in an act of common prayer and worship of the same common God. Now that's the same God worshipped by Pearse, Tone and McCracken.

The Long, Winding and Deadly Roads

I believe that it was a heated discussion on *The Late Late Show* that finally changed government thinking on random breath-testing. There's been fall-out, of course. Rural pubs, already hit by the smoking ban, are now closing at an alarming rate, but perhaps 100 people are alive today who would have died because someone was drinking and driving. At last, something had been done which really did impact on road deaths. At last, there was a measure that could not be perverted into a revenue-gathering scam. The last excuse of the Gardaí was removed. Poor detection figures could no longer be explained away by failings in the law. And the Gardaí have not been lacking. Detection figures have soared; deaths have been dramatically reduced.

I started in RTÉ in 1973 as night editor in the news room, and all night the copy baskets would fill with stories. Too many would be the simple few lines recording the ending of a life on our roads. We all became used to these deaths. No politician wanted any responsibility for the bad news. A toothless safety authority would act as a lightning conductor for those who really did have the power to do something but who listened to spin doctors, sought photo ops and acted on hunches not research and not logic as we'd recognise it. For decades, bad driver training, poor roads, rotten driving and poor enforcement have killed people, but only recently has any of this been acknowledged because to do so was to accept responsibility. I wrote about these things in anger and fear that one day I too would get a phone call from the Gardaí in the early hours of the morning. It's personal.

What's in a hunch?

Broadcast 28 June 2004

Just before the recent batch of elections,[1] I was released back into the community under the supervision of a senior producer. Our mission was to sound public opinion about the issues that concern the man and woman in the street. Now, it became clear that by a ratio of about three to one, top of the list was the cash-gobbling mess that we call our health services. But there was real anger about other things too: smoking bans, affordable housing, decentralisation, the number and condition of our schools – no shortage of issues to provoke a law-abiding population into sharpening up the guillotine and offering free rides on a tumbril to our government politicians.

One persistent irritant was the perception, at least, that an overworked, under-resourced garda force was being diverted from protecting and serving the population to gathering revenue with radar guns on some of the safest roads in the State. Surely this is just an error in perception? All those garda speed traps are saving lives! Well, tragically, they are not. The last bank-holiday figures show that, despite a well-publicised garda blitz on speeding, the grief continued unabated. Other figures don't get trumpeted from the front door of Government

1 The European and local government elections in 2004.

Buildings; they ooze under the back door. They get mentioned in hushed tones, are conjectured in bars – for example, that only about 11 per cent of serious accidents occur on our high-quality roads, constructed for safe, fast driving, whilst about 84 per cent of policing takes place on these roads. 'That proves that policing works', some say. Nonsense. It indicates that the real carnage takes place on the roads neglected by the Gardaí.

The suspicion exists that gardaí are expected to fill quotas, that it is now about cash, a nice little earner. An estimated 150,000 drivers now have penalty points, some with several; say, in all, about 200,000 tickets at 85 euro a pop: that's a great little earner. It's enough to put more gardaí on the streets of our towns and cities, enough to give the Gardaí themselves safer, better cars, to protect them from real criminals. But no, we just paid. The carnage continues, and the people of Ireland don't feel protected from violent crime.

The problem is that we are all guilty from time to time of acting on a hunch. What seems like a good idea appears logical and sensible but does not, in fact, stand close scrutiny. Someone had a hunch that there was widespread devastation being caused by defective vehicles. Because of that hunch, we got the NCT. Commercial vehicles already had strict testing. In fact, only about 3 per cent of accidents were caused by mechanical failure, and there were already strict rules about vehicle safety. Now cash is being extracted from motorists who don't have the county of registration of their car written in Irish in large letters on their number plate. Why? When did you ever hear a coroner announce 'This poor man would be alive today if only he had Port Lairge written on his number plate'? That's not about safety. It's about bureaucracy and cash. So, I have a hunch that a lot of ministerial hunches, encouraged by ambitious civil servants, are unsupported by anything other than the prospect of more photo opportunities.

Speed kills; yes, it can. But a British government think tank showed that it was only the primary cause in 7 per cent of serious accidents. Could it be our hunch is wrong? That we need to apply proper research and good quality thinking? What's the most dangerous time on our roads? Well, between midnight and 3am, we are told. When are you least likely to see a garda? Yes, you have guessed. Who would appear to be statistically most at risk? Our young drivers. But, unlike many of the older generation, they passed the test after professional instruction. Could it be that both the test and the instruction need to be reviewed? One insurance company offers what it calls an ignition course for recently qualified drivers and, after assessment, will offer, they say, up to 50 per cent off their insurance, though I suspect the average is closer to 20 per cent. Well, I know someone who did that one-day course and who was told that much of what they had been taught to pass the test was not best or safest practice. This course is supported by clever actuaries, people in whose interest it is to reduce accidents, and they are saying, officially, 'We are doing it the wrong way.' Rules of the Road, with things like braking distances that haven't been updated for more than thirty years, were lifted straight from the UK. And if the driving test is a real test, with lots of component parts, why not give an overall mark at the end? Let that be the basis for the insurance quotation and a real incentive to learn how to drive and stay alive. Many experts agree that what kills the most is bad driving. On the day you pass your test, you can drive at 75 mph on a motorway without ever having done so before. You now have a piece of paper that says, 'You're safe and you're competent.'

I have a hunch that nothing effective will be done; there is just too much cash coming in and too many measures decided on the basis of a hunch.

Painting by numbers
Broadcast 10 December 2004

As you sit there in the traffic, do you stifle a yawn when you hear the latest statistics on anything at all come up as a news item? Statistics, other than those about other people's sex lives, are not inherently interesting. No, they are mostly poison pellets of misinformation fired into the national psyche to soften us up or persuade us that whatever *we* think, everyone else disagrees, so you 'shut up'. They are not downright lies, but it's hard to believe that, as quoted, they are not designed to deceive.

Did you notice that phrase 'as quoted'? Because most of the figures are accurate, in a way, but most of the conclusions are spun like a good yarn, which is exactly what they are. For example, the Garda Commissioner was asked to comment on the now infamous deployment of gardaí known as 'shooting fish in a barrel'. We've seen it; we know it's the case; but the poor gardaí are now addicted to it. Brownie points for the most successful scalp-hunter, a ten-year-old, barely roadworthy clapped-out saloon for the unproductive, I suppose. Well, the Commissioner pointed out, doubtless with absolute accuracy, that only 3 per cent of speeding penalties were handed out on our motorways. But, Commissioner, much of the hunting grounds for gardaí, too lazy or too scared to find a genuine accident black spot, are dual carriageways and other good safe stretches of road, that are not, strictly speaking, motorways. So the Commissioner told no lies.

Very few people want to do more than the 70 mph[1] our few motorways allow, and on one of them, the M50, that 70 mph is an aspiration – for sixteen hours a day. It's impossible to go faster. So, no lies, but no answer either. The garda addiction to the easy score remains unchecked, even encouraged; meanwhile, of course, crime prospers.

A while back, we were told by a jubilant quango that cigarette-smoking was down 16 per cent. The figures actually refer to cigarette sales. Since when did the island's paramilitaries, smugglers and other gangsters return their sales figures to the Government? There has to be some reduction in cigarette-smoking because of the ban, but 16 per cent? No sir. Millions of cigarettes are sold for half the official price, duty not paid. They are readily available, especially in Dublin and in the border counties. Professor Luke Clancy wanted a 2-euro-a-pack increase in the budget. This would have given the illegals a profit margin akin to heroin, with much smaller penalties. Oh, Brian Cowen is a very shrewd and well-informed man.[2]

Another survey claimed 84 per cent of the Irish population supported the workplace smoking ban. This was interpreted as meaning that 84 per cent supported the ban in pubs. There is a difference. Yes, pubs are someone's workplace, but in the public mind there is a difference, and, anyway, those figures don't stand scrutiny.

---

1 At the time of writing, 2004.
2 Revenue return subsequently showed that cigarette sales were up 8 per cent.

And were those conducting the poll told to avoid licensed premises? A million smokers in Ireland, most of them adults; so who was asked? I hope that all school-children are anti-smoking. So where did the 84 per cent come from? From them? You can expect many more sur-veys and well-spun statistics as a well-funded quango seeks to justify its existence and its substantial budget.

No one is going to commission expensive surveys unless it's in their interest. 'Do you believe the Health Service is a shambles?' Damn right. It's probably close to unanimous, but no official body is going to cut a stick to beat itself. If you hear a survey like that, you have probably been prescribed hallucinogenics by mistake. Anyway, the question would be something like, 'Do you think nurses and doctors are hard-working caring professionals?' And I reckon there'd be a 95 per cent, 'Yes'. I'm fairly certain of that. The official interpretation would be, '95 per cent of the Irish population think they have the best health service in the world.' You get the gist?

Gene Kerrigan in the *Sunday Independent* has drawn attention to that advertisement where you see a tidal wave of litter engulfing a housing estate. It was, of course, a softening-up operation for thumping bin charges, and the ad doesn't mention that only 15 per cent of refuse is domestic. But I suspect that we are expected to pay for more than that!

And, of course, I have to admit RTÉ does it as well. When we are reminded of the undoubted value that you get from a television licence, my morale dips. I know that our senior execs have to wriggle across the Minister's carpet, waving an empty gruel bowl and wailing, 'Please,

Sir, can we have some more?' The difference is that what you see is what you get.

The Government spends the GNP of an emerging nation on spin doctors. And what do we get for those millions? Codded, hoodwinked and annoyed. What are the criteria for employing a government spin doctor? Well, ability to keep a straight face, good suit for the boys, inevitable little black number for the girls, claimed personal relationship and friendship with every influential journo in the town, ability to buy large meals and bottles of grog, ability to hold the aforesaid, professed adoration of employer, high regard for the truth and how to shape it to their employer's advantage.

They know that the results of any poll, survey or report can be preordained by the questions asked. For example, a question, 'Do you think that those charged with administrating the affairs of our nation are entitled, nay bound, to have the very best advice available?' Oh, a 99 per cent 'Yes', I'm sure. Ah, but the extrapolated conclusion by the spin doctor? 'Ninety-nine per cent of the Irish population, including pre-school children, criminal lunatics and the otherwise bewildered, believe that the Government should increase the number of highly paid advisers, if necessary, by paying them buckets more.' Don't laugh: as I say this, some of them will be saying to each other, 'Not a bad idea, why didn't we think of that?' Answer: 'Because you are really not worth the money.'

The buck stops where?

Broadcast 7 January 2005

As you sit there in the evening traffic, do you ever wonder where the buck stops in Ireland? In public administration, a minister very quickly learns to keep a safe distance away from failure or bad news, while still being responsible. Hence, you will see a happy minister opening a new stretch of motorway, waving the official scissors at the camera. But you won't see the same minister posing at a toll-booth to celebrate an outrageous 20 per cent increase in charges that has no justification and is even contrary to the same government's stated policy on prices and inflation.

Are the employees of National Toll Roads currently celebrating a stunning 20-per-cent wage rise? I think not. Do we get a single portaloo, even a lay-by for that increase? No sir. Rafts of regulations and the increased depression of the Irish motorist.

Can we justify it by saying, 'Well, the Minister has saved lots of lives, even if we have suffered a bit?' No, we can't. Road deaths are up 13 per cent, another huge tragic failure.

Will anyone stand up and say, 'We got it wrong'? There is a patent reluctance by ministers to confront the management of the Gardaí. We don't need more regulations; we need the prudent application of the existing regulations by a well-managed force; and we obviously don't have that. One arrest per county per day for drink-driving over Christmas. Is that the best they can do?

Let's look at the measures aimed at reducing deaths. Penalty points: good idea but, of course, debased and rendered nigh-on useless by the garda practice of sitting on the likes of the superb Arklow bypass shooting fish in a barrel, just a few miles from a notorious black spot that remains a garda-free zone. That's bad management.

And when do so many of those accidents occur? After closing time. How many gardaí are deployed on the routes at that hour? Very, very few. Do they have the equipment to check for drugs consumption? Of course not. Are they all equipped with appropriate vehicles? That's another no. Can we possibly see an extra 2,000 gardaí on stream before the next election? Not a prayer.

Are many of our speed limits too high? Yes – and that should be remedied on the 20th when speed limits go metric. Are many ludicrously low, undermining the credibility of the limits? Yes, and that will not be remedied. Indeed, the anonymous local-authority officials who tell the Minister, rather than ask him, what to do, continue to reduce the limits on roads like the Stillorgan dual carriageway, where when it is possible to do 40 mph it is safe to do so. No, these experts are saving lives by reducing the limit by 2½ mph. That will, of course, slow the flow and cause more tailbacks.

The Minister has considerable power, but it never seems to be used to ease the discomfiture or inconvenience of that most persecuted of species, the Irish motorist. Don't forget, the last minister said the speed limits on roads like the Stillorgan dual carriageway were too low.

Well, the local-government officials have shown him who is the boss – they lowered them!

Ministers are also famous for acting on hunches. We were told that we could get a sticker to fit over our old speedometers to convert them to metric. Piffle. There is no universal sticker available, and the cost of converting your speedo between 500 and 1,000 euro. You might have a small inner ring on your speedometer with kph marked in smaller, fainter letters, in which case you might need to drive with bifocals to read it. Implications for safety? Well, think about it.

We are told that fatigue is a growing cause of accidents. Will someone tell the Minister that as the motorway network increases so will fatigue-related accidents, since we don't even have a lay-by on them? Perhaps it's reckoned that the need to use a non-existent toilet will keep us all awake.

The primary cause of accidents is bad driving, not necessarily speed, yet we continue to train our learner drivers to pass the test, not to be safe, courteous drivers. Our data is based on UK figures more than thirty years out of date and despised by the biggest of our motor insurers, who run their own post-test courses. We still ban learner drivers from motorways. Why? Because the British do. Surely motorway experience is essential under supervision?

How many schools use that transition year to teach safe driving? How many trucks, trailers, tractors and diggers have you seen today without number plates or rear lighting? How many overloaded commercials have you travelled behind, wondering about their bald tyres and illegal loads? When did you last see a weighbridge?

Give us a break, Minister, take charge. We don't want to die, or kill, on our roads. Start looking carefully at the data and forget hunches. Start listening, start thinking, because we do know where the buck stops.

Bees under the bonnet

Broadcast 27 January 2007

Now, while the Minister smiled for the cameras, the Gardaí were uttering unveiled threats about the full rigours of the law.[1] No leeway, no understanding, we'll get you, that sort of thing. More fish in more barrels, more revenue. It didn't make me feel particularly well disposed. The official line is that they have no choice. That is not so, the Gardaí have a discretion.

Well, the changeover was a bit ham-fisted, considering the run-up time, and it didn't address the confusing number of different limits. Those limits, in many cases, are sensible, but it's the loony ones that make us despise the poverty of thought that dreams them up. The primary cause of serious – indeed, most – accidents isn't speed. It's bad driving, of which inappropriate speed is only one possible manifestation. Let's not rattle on about that. The PR is wasted if it leaves us feeling hostile and frustrated. Some of those limits, you see, are patently too low. Minister, change them.

What about scoring some serious brownie points with us by addressing some of the things which have actually nothing to do with safety and, indeed, could reduce

1 The occasion was the change from mph to kph and the
adjustment of speed limits.

revenue, but which continue to annoy motorists? For example, number plates. I know of no one who likes that big date stamp on their plate: 97 D, for example, an indication of obsolescence delineating the lowly status of those who can't afford an 05. Hence, millions flow out of the country by those who feel the need to put up a front, sometimes for good reason. Second-hand values are at an all-time low, and it's an offence against ecology to waste so much of our energy and resources. A source of revenue is lost because, unlike our near neighbours, we can't have personal plates. We've got the beastly NCT, so roadworthiness isn't an issue. Those Irish plates cost us thousands in depreciation. Give us a break; at least give us a choice.

Now, you might think that the motor trade love this date-stamped imperative. Well, they don't, because their new-car business dies after just the first quarter of the year. Why register a car, for example, in October, November, December, when it will be worth thousands less a few weeks later? BMW went public; they want to give the best customer service they can and sell their cars over twelve months of the year, but those wretched plates mean too much business is heaped into January, February, March. The argument in favour was that the Gardaí otherwise couldn't work out the registered owner. Even Garda Homer Simpson could manage a few simple letters and numbers! Look, we don't like them, and we would like you a bit more if you got rid of them, or at least gave us the choice.

Here's the big one: road tax. Like most things to do with our driving laws, it's based on thinking and technology that are at least forty years out of date. The bigger your engine, the more you pay, regardless of the fact that many larger engines nowadays are more economical and, indeed, cleaner than some smaller cars. Some of the smaller cars are flying machines and real guzzlers. There are those who genuinely try to curb their use of the car for environmental reasons. So, are they incentivised or rewarded? No sir, they pay the same road tax as a high user. The polluter pays no more than the green user.

The solution seems simple. Bearing in mind that this is a hunch, abolish road tax. What? Yes, abolish road tax and put the tax on fuel so the heavier the use the more you pay. Commercial users get a rebate anyway on their diesel; fuel costs for companies are tax deductible. Economy would be rewarded, profligacy penalised.

We have an incentive to find leaner, greener vehicles and fuels. Eco-taxes would satisfy our international obligations, and I say that as a relatively high-mileage driver. So give the driver the right to choose. If they can find a safe sturdy car with good fuel economy, let them climb in and get out of those flimsy little boxes that offer such little protection and must contribute to the deaths and serious injuries on our roads. If the sums worked out, most of us would love you to bits for that.

On a very rare occasion, I have shared a table at a function with Bertie Ahern, and once, by way of small talk, I ran that one past him. He was, as ever, polite and, as ever, non-committal – but remember: abolishing road tax was one of the promises that gave Fianna Fáil their biggest-ever election victory back in 1977. When I mentioned that, there was a distinct twitch. So, who knows, it wouldn't be the first time a hunch rang a bell. Ah, the bells, the bells.

Cash before climate?

Broadcast 9 September 2005

'There is to be no carbon tax in the foreseeable future.' I have rarely seen a minister react so quickly and so emphatically. Let us sit in our traffic jams and yield a collective sigh of relief. We don't want to be here, of course, in a queue. We are not part of a global conspiracy to bore holes in the ozone layer. We don't want to use global warming to make Kerry part of the hurricane zone, but we don't have much of a choice.

We already give the Government 67 per cent of the price of every litre of petrol we buy, so they have had a huge windfall profit, and, yes, we should conserve energy, especially fossil fuels – but we already pay, listen to it, 51 per cent more than the UK for electricity. What genius thought that we could easily afford more, that our competitiveness wouldn't be affected? Did high taxation curb smoking, drinking – buying cars, for that matter? Find a photograph of Minister Dempsey and light candles in front of it (not oil lamps or electric bulbs, of course).

The search for alternative fuels needs a carrot, not a stick. The Irish taxpayer, and, one way or another, that's all of us, already pays bundles. A year or so ago, I mentioned in one of these columns the suitability of bio-diesel, of oil-seed rape as an alternative to diesel, of the half-million useless acres of Irish farmland lying fallow – that 'set aside' can still be paid on land producing non-food crops. Now we see a worried CIE deciding to experiment with alternatives to regular diesel, and we hear about producing electricity using elephant grass as fuel.

Why has the Government gone cold on wind power? Well, there are two powerful groups who have to be on side: the oil companies and the Department of Finance. Both need to protect their huge vested interests in fuel production. There are those who are back even to talking about coal, which is a particularly dirty fossil fuel and takes an awful lot of cleaning up, but wartime Germany and apartheid South Africa both developed technologies for refining petrol from coal. Things would have to be pretty desperate before those technologies are resurrected.

We do, right now, have clean and plentiful alternatives. We always have had. Liquid petroleum gas is abundant, and it sells in the UK for 31 pence a litre – that's about 50 cent, or less. Gas-conversion kits are now pretty sophisticated; it's a good technology, and the burnt gas produces mostly water. But the Department of Finance here loaded it so much that it wasn't worth converting.

The oil companies didn't put up much of a struggle either because they were going to sell us petrol. So a clean, plentiful alternative was killed off because the Department was protecting revenue, not the environment.

So much official thinking is based on out-moded technology, old, redundant information – we are talking about things like the Rules of the Road, the stopping distances of cars, the way we train our learner drivers and the way we impose tax on cars. So you've got one minister, perhaps, preaching prudence in the purchase of an eco-friendly vehicle and another one sticking on just as much excess taxation as on an unfriendly beast of a car.

We still pay road tax on an ancient assessment of horsepower, when a small hot-rod can guzzle as much gas and put out more pollution than one of those big MPVs or SUVs that's fitted with a modern high-tech diesel. It's true, but the Department of Finance isn't thinking about pollution or conservation; their job, as they see it, is to protect revenue, so it will take a political decision to change it.

I ask again, 'Why do we pay an annual ransom to use roads that fuel, tolls, purchase taxes have already paid for many times over? Of course, one reason is that we have legions of public servants involved in its administration, and we have departments addicted to cash. Oh, and if you have just purchased a car, try reminding your friendly local garda that the reason it's not taxed, and won't be for a while, is that there are an alleged 90,000 documents, like some huge snowdrift, piled high in Shannon, awaiting processing. (Oh yes, if you want to experience infinity, try phoning them!)

So, let's look at the situation, last week, next week, next year, it's not going to change. If you're stuck at a toll-bridge, the Government is getting a big piece of that inaction. The petrol you waste in that traffic jam means more cash for the Government, and when your carved-up car gives up the ghost, buckets of cash for the Government when you buy the new one. Alternative fuels? Over the Department's dead body!

Fianna Fáil went to the Slieve Russell in search of inspiration, while beautiful Belvedere House in Mullingar hosted the wedding breakfast for Fine Gael and

Labour. What I want to hear are their plans, all of them, to make our lives a bit better. I want to know, for example, where all the parties stand on things like alternative fuels, incentives and carbon taxes, because this turkey is not going to vote for Christmas.

Stop the nonsense

Broadcast 24 October 2005

Seeing Dr Tiede Herrema over in Ireland to hand over some of his personal papers brought a lot of memories back. His kidnapping by Eddie Gallagher and Marian Coyle was remarkable by any standards, culminating as it did with the siege of a house in Monasterevin. The full story has never been told, I promise you, even thirty years later. The Garda Press and Information Service was, then, in its infancy. And it could be a little overcautious. BBC kept a clip of their reporter Keith Graves, who now works for Sky, asking a very senior garda, 'What is the situation today?' Came the reply, 'The same as it was yesterday.' 'And what was the situation yesterday', countered Graves. Came the final reply, 'If you don't know that, I'm not telling you.' Ah, those were the days.

Now, of course, there is a regular stream of words from the Garda Press Office, but not always that useful to hard-nosed news hounds. Jim Cusack, and, it seems, all of Independent Newspapers, incurred the wrath of the Office by describing much of the details released to a panting media as 'fluff' – stuff about the success of the garda judo team, and so on, and not enough hard information about crime. Perhaps Cusack's most telling point came after a confrontation on Newstalk 106, when the results of Operation Anvil were discussed. You may recall that Anvil was the 6.5-million-euro crackdown on organised crime, which really doesn't seem to have cracked too many gangsters, but which, the Gardaí boasted, had caught 1,500 motorists for tax or insurance offences. Now, hang on, 6.5 million euro extra for what was routine traffic policing?

Let me make a few things clear. In thirty-two years of journalism this side of the border, I found the overwhelming majority of gardaí decent, honest, dutiful and, yes, compassionate. Many's the young offender had his or her life turned around through the compassionate treatment of a garda. Bereaved families have often spoken about the care and the kindness of even very senior gardaí. There've always been great thief-catchers and men and women of incredible courage, so don't damn an entire force because of what went on in Donegal or because a few thugs, drunks or paedophiles, for that matter, get the headlines. The Gardaí are, for the greatest part, sound.

What you are right to question is the management of the force. Recently on the M50, a senior RTÉ colleague saw a black Mercedes pulling over a speeding car; a friend saw a silver Lexus in action with a blue flashing light; and I personally saw a new, unmarked Toyota Avensis, blue light flashing, tearing along the motorway. So much effort, on the safest and, at rush hour, the slowest road in the State. There are many other roads, such as the heavily patrolled Arklow bypass, and the horrible fatalities that occur at either end on roads that rarely see a garda checkpoint. I bet that there is a superintendent in Donegal who'd give his eye teeth to be able to deploy resources like that on the blood-soaked highways of his county.

So let's stop talking nonsense. The Head of the Road

Safety Council has appeared in print giving vent to his frustration that no one seems to be prepared to take responsibility for road safety. I learned from my radio that car ownership has trebled in thirty years; fatalities have actually fallen a bit over three decades, but the improvements in roads and in car quality have not reflected the drop in fatalities such as they've had in the UK. Driver training here is still in the Dark Ages – not the fault of the Gardaí. Policy and policing show poor deployment, and that is the fault of senior gardaí.

They know, we know, the Minister knows, most fatalities occur between midnight and 3am. Where are the Gardaí then? Drugs saturate the nightclubs, yet there's no test kit issued to screen a driver who might have snorted three or four lines of cocaine, popped E, smoked heroin or cannabis, be full of amphetamines. Random drink-testing is still being 'considered'. Well, you can double, even treble, the traffic corps, but if they're not deployed properly and equipped adequately, it's absolutely useless.

All the time, easy excuses are sought. A tragedy in Donegal, and we hear about the car culture there, the interest in motor sports. What's the excuse in Louth? Meath? There's a great car culture in other parts – Carlow, for example. Why are their figures not so grotesque? We know that bad roads kill. Bad driving, not necessarily illegal speed, is a primary cause. When will someone acknowledge that inappropriate policing makes money, wastes lives? Eddie Shaw is right: someone needs to take charge and take responsibility. In France, President Chirac headed the road-safety initiative. We have a good police force, but very poor deployment. It is frustrating for gardaí, and it can be tragic for others.

Belling the cats

Broadcast 5 December 2005

I've been thinking about managers. When I started working for the BBC as a freelance trainee, the lowest possible life form, some thirty-seven years ago, management had many tiers. A producer in charge of reporters was, by definition, a manager who taught, motivated, was a conduit for ideas and was custodian of the BBC ethos. These producers were answerable to divisional heads and so on up the clearly defined pyramid.

RTÉ works in a similar system and so, I suspect, do most large organisations. They are not democracies or communes. They might consult, but somewhere along the line, someone has to take a decision, and subordinates have to try and implement it. Someone has to take responsibility.

Over the years, for me, the best managers were those who took clear, unambiguous decisions. I might not necessarily have agreed, might indeed have argued, but at least there was a clear instruction from someone who would take responsibility for it. It seems to me now that across the public sector the management art is to be visible but unaccountable.

On a recent radio programme, a distinguished academic, who actually teaches managers, seemed to argue that hospital hygiene was the responsibility of the workers, not the managers, when, of course, both have duties.

But the mindset worried me – 'I've bought the soap, it's up to you to use it.' No, someone has to take responsibility, to teach, motivate and make sure that there is implementation.

It seems to me that there is a culture of ducking and weaving. The politicians' instinct, of course, is to be Teflon-coated so no criticism sticks. It's so refreshing then, when Professor Drumm, the Head of the Health Service Executive, said recently, 'The buck stops here.' I was shocked: a senior public-service manager who wasn't ducking and weaving.

Look at the waste of public money on a wide range of projects, from computer programs to motorways, and try to find anyone who was in charge at the time. Try to find out who was there, who was in that place where the buck is meant to stop. Peer through the mist if you will, you're wasting your time.

There is a management culture based on *not* taking responsibility, which brings me in a roundabout way to Eddie Shaw, the former Head of the Road Safety Council. I've always liked Eddie and agreed with the aims of his council to reduce deaths and injuries but found that I couldn't agree with their willingness to accept whatever measures government ministers would come up with, and, of course, eventually Eddie couldn't either and he quit.

His many criticisms of government policy focused on a central point that no one was prepared to take responsibility for road safety. Eddie could only advise and urge but actually had no power. The existence of the Road Safety Council is, in fact, 'a fudge' – something that gave the impression that something was being done, something that insulated ministers and senior gardaí from responsibility. Eddie Shaw never complained, but I know that the job paid buttons. An agency deckhand would have been better paid. That was a measure of how Government valued the job.

The management of the Gardaí, in relation to road safety, is preposterous. But road safety takes in roads; now, that's a different minister. Transport; oh, that's another one. Finance has a role; oh, that's another minister. No one who could be called the Minister Responsible for Road Safety. No one takes responsibility.

Oh yes, look out for that phrase, 'Road Safety is the responsibility of every one of us.' That truism is another cop-out, another fudge. There are lots of things that the individual cannot control: the quality of roads, the eccentric policing, the inadequate public-transport system, the absence of random breath-testing, the poor and inappropriate training for learner drivers. There's a long list.

And what about sentencing? Light up a cigarette in a pub, and there is a 3,500-euro fine, but a drunk driver who slaughters two entirely innocent people gets a 2,000-euro fine. What's the message there? Oh, there's much hand-wringing, lots of photo opportunities and a tidal wave of grief. Christmas is coming, and the undertakers will be busy, but across the Administration, the cry will accurately state, 'Road safety? That's not my department.'

Motorists anonymous

Broadcast 12 December 2005

My name is Derek, and I'm addicted to motor cars.

I also know an awful lot of people in the motor trade, but if you go to lunch with two of them, there is a kind of moaning competition as each relates the misery of trying to make money. I have been so moved, I've not only paid for the lunch, but I've been tempted to offer them a couple of quid for a bag of coal and a pair of shoes. Yet, they all seem to be surviving quite nicely because you, the customer, will buy 170,000 new cars this year and thousands upon thousands of second-hands. In short, the trade is buoyant.

Prime Time revealed that illegal price-fixing was widespread, to your detriment, with dealers penalised if they sold below an agreed bottom line; illegal and inexcusable. There is anecdotal evidence that some dealers would break ranks to undercut, especially another brand.

Well, at least you know from the outset the approximate price of a new car and, because it's new and unused, it carries some sort of warranty for a period. The dealer has a margin improved by a substantial kickback from a finance company, probably, and further enhanced by bonuses from the importer-distributor based on the number of cars the dealer sells.

By and large, most people realise all that, but what isn't roared from the rooftops is the biggest cost to you.

It's not finance, not fuel, nor even maintenance or insurance. It's depreciation – what's called 'residual value' – and dealers who have overestimated that have been scalded while you, the customer, take your own bath.

The best of cars will drop 50 per cent of their new value in three years, and some very good, very well-built cars can drop that much in twelve months. Why, and how would you know? Well, if the model you are buying is due to be replaced, depreciation will be all the greater when the new model comes out. And if a model has proved popular with company fleets, hire companies and other big-volume buyers, when they hit the market as second-hands, the market becomes glutted, and the value of each car is forced down.

There are fields of unsold trade-ins around the country. By and large, there is little wrong with them except there are too many of them, and that can cost you thousands. Of course, the other side of that coin is that if you are buying second-hand, someone else has lost those thousands, and the dealer might be anxious to blow it out the door at cost or less just to realise the profit on the new car against which he took the trade-in.

It's never been a better time to buy second-hand, but the phrase 'buyer beware' has greater than ever significance. *Prime Time* highlighted the widespread fraud known as 'clocking' – that's turning back the recorded mileage. Up to 1992, you could look at the ownership document, which was a heavy cardboard book, and see the name and address of previous owners. You could check the history.

That information still exists in Shannon, but you can't access it. The NCT has a record of the mileage at the car's last test, but, of course, you can't access it. The

Government could, at a stroke, make that information available, but it is, it seems, interested only in revenue, about 40 per cent of the new price, in fact. Consumer protection? Mmm, it doesn't seem so.

You should know, though, that the computer-management system on many modern cars can be interrogated by an expert to determine the real mileage, even if the display has been altered, and a service record should also show recorded mileage.

What about badly damaged cars, glued back together again but still un-roadworthy? The insurance companies have the claims history of every car on their computers. Ha ha, guess what? You can't access it. Stolen cars: they are all on the garda computer, but, of course, they won't tell you. Cars on which finance payments are still due and therefore cannot be sold legally, well, you can find that out through a couple of specialist companies, but, by and large, officialdom doesn't give two hoots about consumers. You are on your own out there.

There is a glimmer of light because the public aren't the only ones caught by rogue cars. Dealers lose money and reputation when someone dumps a lemon on them, and they are driving on a system with a British agency called Experian, which will be piloted by the motor trade next year and will give dealers access to all those secret details: ownership, mileage, crash history, credit history; and the plan is to extend this service online to the public. For a small fee, HPI in the UK can do that for all UK cars. If the Government does give two hoots, it will make it possible here. But remember the message: you are on your own; and if the deal seems too good to be true, it is.

Update

The situation has improved, and a range of checks is available, if you know where to look. The best advice may be had from organisations like the AA.

The empty chairs

Broadcast 23 December 2005

I have enjoyed a brief period of uncharacteristic broadcasting activity. I was one of Vincent Brown's studio guests discussing the great and the good, the famous and infamous who had died during 2005. Fergus Sweeney had compiled an alarmingly long list, and there were a couple of old friends on it. One was the artist, Gerald Davis. I was sorry we didn't get around to discussing his life and work, because it was a life filled with art and music and optimism, a life fulfilled. Everyone on Fergus's list had made their mark far beyond their own circle of friends and relatives.

My next engagement was a piece on *The Late Late Show* about road-accident deaths. There were two women on the panel who had lost children in road accidents – bright, much-loved young people whose potential was never fulfilled. The waste of those lives burned. There were two gardaí in the studio as well, unable, because of protocol, to voice the frustration of the force at how poorly equipped they are to deal with drinking and driving. There is no point in reprising the whole piece, since most of you would probably have seen it (*The Late Late Show*'s ratings are huge; there were about 800,000 watching that night), but even with that generous slot, not everything that should have been said got said.

In the past ten years, more people have died on the roads of the Republic than have lost their lives in thirty years of the Troubles – here, in the North and in Britain. It's running at about 400 a year. That's one jumbo-jet-load a year. Now, you would think that with that kind of attrition rate, road deaths would attract the highest-quality thinking, priority in the drafting of legislation and ruthless enforcement. Well, think again.

Let's look at that. Less than 2 per cent of accidents were caused by mechanical failure, but still we got the NCT. Seemed like a good idea at the time, even if there was little research to support it. But, at least, we can be fairly sure that the cars are in pretty good shape. Most serious accidents occur not in the heavily policed motorways and dual carriageways but on that tangled web of bad roads which are harder to police and which, anyway, yield fewer rewards for the garda in need of detections. At last, and at least, a minister has acknowledged that bad roads kill, and the roads, like the cars, are improving.

But here's the thing: the accident figures aren't. So, if the cars and the roads are improving, why do the deaths continue to rise? The answer is us, the drivers. The primary cause in most fatal accidents is bad driving, driver error: 88 per cent of fatal accidents. It's not necessarily speed. That accounts for just 13 per cent. All of that calls for a number of urgent measures.

Driver training is uneven, and it focuses only on passing the test, not necessarily being a good, courteous, careful road-user with the skills to cope with every likely eventuality. We are building more motorways, but theoretically, and legally, our learner drivers can't use them until they have passed their tests, so they have no training or testing at speed. We are stuck with old British criteria, thirty years out of date, and instructors who don't require, by law, any formal training to teach.

Even with good training, car and road accidents will happen, but there is one factor that plays a part in killing about 120 people a year, and that's alcohol; and that's something you, the Gardaí and the legislators can act on. You can act by leaving the car at home when there is even the chance of a drink. You can act by stopping your friends, whose judgement is impaired, from getting into their cars; by not applauding the hard man who drives home after a rake of pints; and by using your phone to inform, if need be. Now that goes against the Irish psyche, but if you thought someone was going out to commit a murder or molest a child, you would. Well, you could be saving the driver's, passenger's or someone else's life by getting a drunk off the road.

The Gardaí can help by improving their miserable detection rates and deploying with greater logic, but, most of all, those photo-loving legislators could review the shreds of the Road Traffic Act and make acquittals on a technicality a thing of the past. Convictions have been halved in three years because of loopholes. There is, in the history of the State, no more-challenged legislation.

Above all, there must be random breath-testing, lots of it. But the bleat from the Department is that, 'it might be unconstitutional, you know, we are actually not sure, well, we haven't actually done anything about it.' We have had thirty-four constitutional amendments; one more won't hurt, and all the evidence screams that it will save lives, so for God's sake, get on with it.

If you happily take a drink and drive, don't be surprised if your children do the same. If you plan to pour drink into your pals this Christmas, make sure that you also get them home. Make sure your children know what to do, how to get home if they have too much to drink. I'd rather get a call at 3 o'clock in the morning asking for a lift home than that dreadful third-party voice telling me that someone will never be coming home – another life cut short, potential unfulfilled, another empty chair this Christmas, hearts broken.

Have a happy, responsible Christmas, make it to the next one.

Fish in a barrel

Broadcast 30 January 2006

Well, the trumpets sounded, and a chorus of officialdom chirped up, 'We have been listening', and here are another thirty-one opportunities for you to lose your driving licence. And, what's more, you remember that line about random breath-testing being unconstitutional? Well, the Attorney General has changed his mind. You *can* have random breath-testing – about six years after it was promised! All it took was a change of mind, and there is more to prove that we listen to *Five Seven Live* and Eddie Shaw.

Eddie was the Chairman of the National Safety Council who had to resign before officialdom took him seriously. Eddie complained that no one with real power was responsible for road safety, despite the fact that the death rate on the roads was rising against international trends. Now there is to be a road-safety group, including the Ministers for Transport, Justice, Health and Education, and Martin Cullen himself will be in charge of progress in road safety. The squeal of brakes you hear is the buck stopping on a ministerial desk, and it's all to be welcomed! The next sound you hear is the light thump of a tiny bouquet from me landing on the same desk. The bouquet would have been bigger and more fragrant if the measures just announced had been brought in earlier, but better late than never. And they are to be welcomed, especially random breath-testing. About 120 people die each year because someone was drinking. That must stop.

The original Séamus Brennan proposals had included a two-point offence for having a bulb out. That simply wasn't fair. The driver has no control over the life expectancy of a bulb and, thankfully, that seems to have disappeared from the schedule of penalty points, and that was important. You see, the offences must be fair. It's not just that unfair regulation would make the Minister and his colleagues as popular as a Chinese chicken with a cough, it's because unfair and unreasonable rules bring the whole code into disrepute. The new regulations, on paper, seem fair, reasonable and desirable. The problem, of course, will be enforcement.

With just three offences carrying points up to now, it became clear that the fish-in-a-barrel syndrome gripped the Gardaí. It seemed their priority became the prosecution of motorists while losing sight of the stated aim of the penalty points: to save lives, prevent accidents. Hence, the safest roads saw the most garda activity. The figures from the Gardaí themselves indicated that 28 per cent of the fatalities occurred on two weekend nights in the wee small hours when policing was at its thinnest. That must be addressed.

Bad driving, the cause of more than 80 per cent of accidents, will now be a punishable offence or, at least, a fairly comprehensive range of thirty-four examples of it. Welcome it, but don't think that that's where it should end.

It's interesting to see that Mary Hanafin, the well-regarded Minister for Education, is on the new Road Safety Committee. But this is the same minister who was distinctly cool on the suggestion that schoolchildren should be taught to drive, should be taught safety as part of their transition year.

We have been promised new Rules of the Road, but who is addressing driver training? Why follow those old UK criteria? I believe that on low-speed roads learner drivers should be allowed, after instruction, to drive unaccompanied, if certified by a registered and qualified driving instructor. I also believe that learner drivers must be given time, accompanied, on our growing motorway network. At the moment, the madness persists that at, say, 10 o'clock in the morning, a learner driver has theoretically never driven at 120 kilometres per hour. One hour later, perhaps, with a driving test passed, that driver can safely put the pedal to the metal, unaccompanied and with no legally obtained experience.

Let's be fair, the politicians have, albeit slowly, taken an important step towards greater road safety, but if enforcement isn't up to the job, it will all be useless, and it's just a step along a long road. We have a traffic corps whose success must be measured not in convictions or in penalties handed out but in compliance, in the reduction of deaths. Bad enforcement has led to a huge rift between the Gardaí and the public. The traffic corps could go a long way to healing that. The important thing is lives saved, not scalps on the totem pole, and that means that their deployment must be kept under regular review. They now have random breath-testing and a whole new array of offences. The politicians have armed them; time will tell if they use all those wonderful new weapons to save lives or shoot themselves in the foot!

It's all about the cash

Broadcast 3 February 2006

Maybe I'm getting a bit confused after thirty-three years in RTÉ, much of it spent trying to make sense of official-dom. Perhaps mixed messages eventually damage the brain. It's either that or conclude that we are frequently lied to, and that, of course, is unthinkable. You see, like thousands of others, I signed up for the new 'pay as you dump' bin service. Not only that, my household dili-gently separates glass by colour, plastics, paper, cans and much more. My local authority diligently separates me from a lot of money, because I'm being good!

Well, lots of you are in the same situation, being good and conscientious, not dumping illegally or polluting, and the reward for many of you: increased charges. What? Yes. Because not enough people are paying up, the diligent fools are being charged more. All that waffle about the environment, all that lying spin, it turns out it's all about cash. When we should be rewarded, we are penalised; and those who don't pay on principle or because they just don't give a hoot can slap their thighs and shout 'Sucker!' at us. They are the ones who are being incentivised.

The same bizarre mixed messages are being received by motorists. You see, we are told that the motorways are the safest roads in the country. The figures support that. Keep traffic, especially heavy traffic, out of towns and residential areas, and lives will be saved. Yet, the biggest, most important ring road in the country is to be infested with tolls, to catch those who don't currently go through the present preposterous toll barrier. There are Scandinavian folk tales about ugly trolls who block river crossings – troll-roads, I suppose – demanding a tribute from all who would pass. Of course, in the stories, the troll is eventually vanquished by a valiant and ingenious hero. Hans Christian Anderson and the like don't mention in a postscript that the mythical hero then set up a system where travellers would be mugged at more regular intervals. That's because, even in a fairytale, that would be unbelievable and unacceptable.

I'm not against toll roads in principle, but the motorist needs to see more than just a barrier. Well-maintained service areas, broad free-flowing highways, long intervals between tolls, some value for money. Ring roads are different. Instead of incentivising drivers to stay out of city roads and streets, we penalise them for using our congested and distinctly unattractive M50. Once again, all the high talk about making the streets safe is just so much cant, because cash takes priority over lives.

Use the bus, use the Dart, the train, the Luas – our public-transport system can't cope. More and more quality bus lanes are appearing even where no buses run, despite the fact that these are a hugely wasteful use of road space and appear to be stuck in willy-nilly, as if there were brownie points in just having them. We don't have an integrated system, we have a collection of independent transport empires. Without a huge increase in suburban park and ride and a similar increase in the number of trains, buses and routes, we will continue to have too many people who have no choice but to use their motor cars. There is no permission for vehicles with three or more occupants to use those bus lanes, yet this could radically increase car-pooling and traffic flow. We would be incentivised, not penalised.

It's too soon to be talking about congestion charges for the cities because they only work when people are incentivised to use public transport instead. A viable alternative to the commuter must be available or it's just a crass and cynical fundraiser. But it's not too soon to go back and look at the professed priorities. Number 1: to save lives. If you penalise those who use the safest roads in the State, you are a hypocrite. If you want traffic volume to be reduced, you incentivise car-sharing and build car parks near the rail heads and suburban bus stops. You stop spinning long enough to listen.

For example, to use the Luas for half a day's shopping in town for two or three people works out just as dear as driving in and paying the ransom in a city-centre car park. Where is the incentive?

In the UK, grants and low duty have encouraged tens of thousands, maybe hundreds of thousands, of drivers to switch to liquid petroleum gas, a very clean, efficient fuel. In the UK, it's less than half the price of petrol, but not here, because revenue takes precedence over the environment and public health. So listen, forget all the professed commitments to save lives and protect the environment: cash is king. Officialdom keeps urging you to save lives and protect the environment; of course, you keep paying.

Passing the driving test, failing as a driver

Broadcast 31 March 2006

I wish Gay Byrne luck with his new Chairmanship of the Road Safety Authority. He has a long record as someone who has led some of the most successful teams in Irish broadcasting and has a well-developed nose for humbug. He is autocratic, bully-proof, a master of the pertinent question. In short, he is ideal to cut through the wall of reports, the mountains of paper that dedicated public servants use to divert and isolate those imposed upon them. It's called sand-bagging. The new top dog is given a bone to chew, then choked with reams of paper. Bad luck boys, that won't work for long!

The bone on offer is driving tests. Over 400,000 drivers are on the road without a full licence, and figures indicate that they are involved in a disproportionate number of accidents, but nothing I have seen suggests more fatalities. Most of those 400,000 are young drivers, and it's not possible to say if it is youth, bad training or inexperience that makes them more accident-prone. Probably a bit of all three.

Simply testing them with the present criteria will improve very little. In short, the present test proves only that for less than an hour a candidate can manoeuvre at low speed. It was devised in 1964. Have you ever driven a car made in the early 1960s? Well, it's all changed: the ride, the handling, the brakes, most of the roads – indeed, the traffic volume – all changed. Only that test remains unchanged after forty-two years, albeit with a simple theory module. But the practical? You might as well toss candidates in the canal: if they float, they pass; if they drown, they fail. It's quicker, cheaper and just about as relevant.

No motorway testing – in fact, no testing at speed – and still 46 per cent fail. That fail rate compounds the backlog, waiting times extend to infinity. A block on civil-service recruitment helps to keep the number of testers down, but reducing waiting times won't improve driving, it will only reduce the waiting time. Think about it: the real safety issue is competence, not the availability of testing, using criteria as old as the Mark I Cortina.

Listen Gay, we have no, repeat *no* certified instructors because no system of certification exists. Any of us with a licence can become a driving instructor. The driving schools teach pupils to pass that antiquated test. That's all. There is no legal requirement to have any lessons at all.

I have some modest suggestions that might improve things. First, revise the criteria for the test to bring it into the twenty-first century, and that includes driving at more than 50 kph (30 mph). It means lifting the ban on motorway driving. Test and certify anyone who wants to be an instructor and allow those certified testers offer a suitable course to certify a pupil as safe to drive alone. Increase your testers then by recruitment.

You must convince Mary Hanafin that safe-driving theory, at least, be part of the transition year for pre-Leaving Cert pupils. Of course, good driving requires more than the ability to drive safely; it requires the right attitude and awareness, and it requires those who should lead by example to do so. If you routinely drive in a dangerous and discourteous way, constantly fuming about that muppet in the car ahead who is holding you back by driving at the legal limit, don't be surprised if your young and impressionable passenger grows up to be just as big a hound on the road as you are. If you impress your children by showing off your abilities to tailgate, overtake to gain a second or two, cut up other drivers, you could be teaching them how to kill themselves or someone else. You see, some of it is not down to Martin Cullen or Gay Byrne, it's down to you.

I don't think that identifying a problem is the answer. Four hundred dead bodies a year, an avalanche of grief, the end of hope. No, we know what the problem is, but just testing and failing or passing learners is not an answer when that antiquated system of poor training and inappropriate testing exists.

The civil servants will come up with lots of reasons why the test can't be changed: 'It might take longer', 'Oh, we might have to relocate the test centres, or something, employ even more testers, retrain the ones we have.' It's all poppycock, 400 bodies a year say it's poppycock. Training won't improve until testing improves. Why should it? The trainers won't improve until you make them. Shortening the waiting lists will only earn the Minister a few brownie points, but until training and testing leave the era of the Hillman Hunter behind, you won't save a single life.

Masters of the U-turn

Broadcast 3 November 2006

I am living proof, though just about, that the common cold is incurable. But bad driving *is* curable. The most difficult of manoeuvres a driver must master could be described as the three-point turn, but those who legislate on driver behaviour, for them, the most difficult is the U-turn. How do you tell the public that you are wrong, a victim of the quick-fix mentality?

A while back, the National Roads Authority declared that rest and service areas on our motorway network were unnecessary – this despite their extensive and, I suspect, expensive travels abroad to see how Johnny Foreigner does it.

Clearly, those who conducted the research were equipped with a unique personal drainage system, incredible stamina and vehicles that required no fuel at all. Quite rightly, a bit late in the day, the Minister told them to reconsider their decision. Now, that's ministerial speak for, 'Catch yourselves on. Go away and construct rest areas.'

The experts were already suspicious that a large number of fatalities had fatigue as their primary cause; now they reckon that perhaps 20 per cent of deaths are caused by driver fatigue. Last year in Ireland, that would have meant eighty lives. And even though the NRA have said they have identified a dozen possible locations –

nothing precise, mind you – we have yet to see even a decent lay-by. So, that's 20 per cent.

Oh, what about illegal speeding? The latest figures are British and just about four weeks old. What would you say then, 50 per cent? No, just 5 per cent. An even smaller number have mechanical failure as their cause. The majority are caused by bad driving – driver error – but the authorities are locked into their fixation with speed. It's not to be ignored, but to concentrate so much effort into the campaign against speed is to lose sight of plain old bad driving. That's what kills more drivers, passengers and pedestrians than anything else. Bad driving.

We have been talking about driver education for more than two years on this programme and the unacceptably long delays for testing because the number of testers and test centres didn't keep pace with the number of cars. We have already pointed out that the criteria for our test are forty years old. A driver is required only to manoeuvre for about half an hour at low speed in a built-up area and, mind you, nearly half of them fail even that. Despite instructions to the contrary, some testers still fail an applicant because, they said, the applicant didn't slow down using the gear box in the old way.

Despite promises, there are still no official qualifications for becoming a driving instructor. Anyway, there is no requirement to have taken lessons in the first place! There is no legal way to have acquired motorway experience. Instead, we get hot under the collar because a lot of people on a provisional licence are driving unaccompanied. Well, I have some modest proposals, which I know, of course, will be ignored.

They start with a core of officially certified instructors, who, after a number of lessons, may certify a learner driver as competent to drive unaccompanied, at no more than 80 kph, mind, and to drive on motorways accompanied by a qualified driver. A learner must get motorway experience before qualification and should be certified motorway competent, or at least 100-kph competent, by an instructor before sitting the official test. You see, the key is instruction, and that starts with the instructor. A driver's log, with appropriate stamps from a certified instructor, should be proof of instruction.

There are lots of reasons why we resist change. We keep looking to Britain, whose own road network is in a mess but where there is, depending on the area, at least some concept of proper enforcement. It's time we realised that we are actually an independent country, that speed cameras in the UK are great for revenue but don't seem to stop accidents.

It's the same mindset that in another area sends those requiring medical treatment to the UK when an infinitely better standard and system exists in France. Our legislators and standard-setters, it seems, have carefully cherry-picked only the rotten cherries from the UK and have ignored the good ones – their airport planning and their metropolitan transport systems.

We have a system that doesn't need tweaking. It needs radical reform and good thinking. If eighty people die because of driver fatigue, stop the guff and start building rest areas. If there are accident black spots, for God's sake, fix the roads. Three years to widen the M50 with one eight-hour shift working per twenty-four hours. Is that really prioritising? Stop talking about better driver education. Do something about it – and, oh yes, give the Gardaí credit for reducing accident rates in their divisions and not for the number of scalps lifted on the safest roads in the State.

Driving? I'll live with the guilt

Broadcast 17 November 2006

Why should you feel guilty about driving your car? If commuters had an easy alternative, they'd take it. And if you'd ever waited for a bus in Dublin's commuter belt, you'd know that thousands of people do. They do use public transport. Even though there's been billions invested, it's not enough, as commuters have to travel greater and greater distances. Our public systems are completely uncoordinated, unintegrated and almost perversely make little provision for those who have to reach a bus or a rail line by car.

Almost every other country I've visited has made huge provision for car parking near its public network, but not here. There is a big, mostly choked, car park for the Luas at Sandyford and a large expensive car park near the Dart in Dun Laoghaire. There are some fairly small car parks near the old stations, but mostly drivers have to abandon on residential avenues or just say 'to Hell with it' and drive on in to work.

The cheapest, most effective way of beating congestion is to treat bus and rail termini as giant 'park and ride' facilities, but one group of local councillors is opposing even a modest car park for a proposed new Dart station near Shankill in County Dublin. Are they mad? No, just trapped by dogma, a dogma that says, 'the car is evil.' These are the people who call for eco-taxes on fuel, as if you had a choice, as if the Government didn't already take more than two-thirds of the price of a litre of fuel, about 67 cent in every euro, as if we didn't already have punitive car taxes and little enough to show for them after decades of extortionate rates.

There are those who object to the road-building programme, and, even though fresh tolls mean that the motorist gets nothing for nothing, the objections continue. Much of the righteous indignation against car-ownership is generated by city-dwelling folk who do have alternatives, but rural and even suburban dwellers have very little choice. Without the private car, there would be huge problems for industry and a crisis in housing. So stop feeling guilty. Most modern diesels are cleaner than even medium-sized petrol engines. A lot of those big SUVs are actually quite green, and a lot of Irish drivers would jump at the choice offered to UK drivers of cheap, very, very clean liquid petroleum gas, about 50 cent a litre in the UK but taxed to extinction here. The truth is, most Irish drivers just want the safest, most comfortable vehicle they can afford to carry themselves and their families.

I'll say something else that's contrary to PC dogma. Cars can be fun. I don't mean exhilarating but irresponsible speed, though motor sport has its place. I mean the liberation of going for a drive – a game of golf, football, a visit to a scenic area, a boot full of fishing rods, a meal in a country restaurant, activities to which public transport doesn't lend itself easily.

If you work hard for most of the week, feel no guilt at a leisurely outing; otherwise, you may as well be on the assembly line of an old Soviet tractor factory. There may be a revelation at the end of even a fairly short trip. For example, a recent trip to Newry brought with it a dramatic political revelation. Newry is a hive of commercial activity, a remarkable shopping venue, but, in and around it, more restaurants and bistros than you would believe, and everywhere fresh paint, new shops, optimism. The local catering college is graduating about seventy chefs a year; the new motorway access across the border more than halfway built. All of that from one trip because, you see, sitting in a car for an hour or so can broaden more than your backside, it can work wonders for the mind.

The Green Shoot

I'm as guilty as most of reminiscing. In most lives, there is much good. We have lived and loved. There have been glorious days in the sun, trips to remember, excitement and friendship. But we have an ability to submerge misery once it's past. Parents tell children about saving the hay, picnics at the beach and the simple treats of childhood. We shelter the younger ones, at least, from the miseries of the past. I was well grown before hearing how TB cut a swathe through my parents' generation. The horrors of the depression in the 1930s are still not fully acknowledged. For me, like the Second World War, this was all ancient history. But not for my parents.

I've lived through some miserable years too and have enjoyed some great times. When we look back with regret at the good times past, we are often mourning the loss of our own vigour and youth – the loss of our optimism. It clouds our judgement. The benefits of prosperity are many; the joys of poverty are few.

We shouldn't let nostalgia distort our view. We have gained a lot, but lost a bit too. Aspiration has driven us to work harder and longer, sometimes at the expense of family life and a sense of community. I have no hesitation in acknowledging the failures of society today, but

when you look at the credit and debit columns of past
and present, I have seen both and know that the present
is better. I believe, with care the future could be much,
much better.

Tears at the airport

Broadcast 24 April 2005

You might think that the life of a newsroom reporter is an exciting and challenging one, and maybe it is now, but thirty years ago, there was an awful lot of boring, grinding routine. Calls to Garda Communications, Shannon Marine Rescue, the RUC and British Army – just to check if anything at all was happening. There were a few correspondents, but no stars and very, very little foreign travel. In fact, things got so tight in the 1970s that at one point only the Director General could authorise a marking abroad, and travel west of Lucan, north of the airport, south of Bray, was severely restricted. The RTÉ car park looked like a breaker's yard, with ageing, crumpled and rusting Hillman Hunters, Ford Cortinas and dying Escorts. I knew a high-profile colleague who owned just one pair of old, cracked shoes. All but a very few with private means or some family money struggled. I can recall just one senior manager in the newsroom ever owning a new car – and a very small one at that.

When the tanker *Betelgeuse* blew up, killing fifty men in Bantry Bay, I was called in at 1 o'clock in the morning to coordinate the cover, and, in fairness, whatever funds were necessary were released. But there was a bank strike. And when, next morning, I was ordered down to Bantry, in a busy newsroom only a deputy chief sub on radio had 25 pounds in cash to get me down there.

The annual Christmas homecoming, joyful and emotional, was easy to cover. There was really only one airport at the time – that was Dublin – with that kind of traffic, and, besides, we needed special permission to go any further. After Christmas, there was a marking, an assignment that we all dreaded. It was the departure again of the economic exiles: young men and women clinging tearfully to their mothers, and big, bony, red-faced farmers from the Midlands and West turning away after a brief handshake, turning to hide their tears.

We saw it year after year, and we accepted that that was the way it was. There were no jobs here, no future. We raised our children for export, and ageing parents went home to the isolation and insecurity of an old age spent without the company of their children.

Rural Ireland was worst. Summers could be lively, hundreds of local festivals to bring those émigrés home again, just for a week or two, and then more tears – until Christmas.

Now, thankfully, so much has changed. There are jobs; there is real prosperity. Infrastructure, of course, couldn't keep up with the pace of it; the Health Service is still a shambles; but that prosperity, for most, is real.

Rural Ireland, however, can still break hearts. Inflated property values still drive out the children of both town and country, and, until very recently, even a farmer with land had difficulty giving a site for his children to build a home, that on family land. Well, the Government may have eased the situation very considerably. Up to now, 70 per cent of those planning applications failed. An increasingly aged and vulnerable population still ache to have their children close.

There are those city folk who regard rural Ireland as a theme park: great to visit, but you wouldn't actually want more than a holiday there. There are genuine concerns about the quality of design, concerns easily addressed. But a lot of our so-called 'vernacular architecture' is slimy, grey slate, grim and depressing. Over-ground electricity is cheap to install and easy to cost. If postal services are overstretched, let them collect it from the post office. The reason underground water (aquifers) get polluted by human effluent is badly installed and poorly managed septic tanks. The answer: inspect them properly. There are no insurmountable problems. Ours is a very sparsely populated country. The population of West Clare, for example, is only one-tenth of what it was before the Famine. There is plenty of room for everyone. There is no need, anymore, for tears at the airport.

How many *fáiltes* will that be?

Broadcast 14 October 2005

When I was growing up in County Down, I worked in bars and hotels for extra cash in the school holidays. There were no age restrictions then on who could work, and it was the kind of education a fee-paying boarding school couldn't provide. I was fortunate. The Old Inn, Crawfordsburn, was a pretty classy place. The food was excellent; top chefs worked there; and Herbie the Sommelier was generous with his knowledge of fine wines. There were beautiful gardens, elegant decor, a big trade in afternoon tea, especially from ladies who drank from the fine china with their little finger carefully extended. At quite a young age, I developed an interest in haute cuisine and good wine but, strangely, perhaps, a distaste for drunkenness. I appreciated the modest wages and the very generous tips.

This was a place popular on the home market and successful in attracting upmarket tourists. I met Paul Mellon, then one of the richest men in the world. Somewhere I have the autograph of John le Carré. Stars of stage and screen passed through, curious and generous Americans – who took mayonnaise on their sandwiches! Even after I had moved on, and the Troubles started, the Old Inn prospered, though, of course, there were fewer tourists.

Moving south of the border in the early 1970s, I was admiring of the value offered by the bed-and-breakfast houses and the accessibility of Irish tourism for even those on modest incomes. I came to know, through friends, the value of tourism to individual households and, indeed, to entire regions. We had a broad spectrum of accommodation and food. After agriculture, it was our most important industry. B&Bs and part-time work put children through college.

Bord Fáilte played a blinder. Continentals were lured to Ireland with great fishing, shooting, equestrian events, superb fresh seafood at reasonable prices. The airlines decanted droves of Americans onto tour buses. Aer Lingus marketing was pretty hot too. The English, especially those with cars, rolled off the ferries. Ireland was a great place to visit.

And I fervently believe that it still is, but tourism now seems to be low on the official agenda. It's being left, it seems, to cut-price airlines to promote. Though Fáilte Ireland still tries hard, tourism no longer holds a privileged place in our priorities.

We have got more money now, and that's good. We have become greedy, and that's not so good. I rarely use B&Bs anymore because I can get a hotel room for much the same money.

For example, on three consecutive occasions, some colleagues and I booked single rooms with an advertised supplement then of about 5–7 euro for single occupancy, only to be charged double because, they said, there were two beds in each room! One landlady in County Louth charged an extra 2½ per cent because I paid with a credit card. Poor food is routinely too dear, so is alcohol, of course, and a lot of trade has been nannied out of existence.

The totality of the smoking ban – look, please, don't shoot the messenger, talk to the publicans – well, that's hit the pubs pretty hard, and they were a major tourist attraction. And the kiddie curfew, even for quite mature teenagers with their parents, has ruined a lot of family holidays. Sea-angling has been wiped out by inshore trawling, which is worth much less than sea-angling tourism. Salmon-angling tourism is on its knees, largely because of over-exploitation, drift-netting. Pollution, most of it agricultural, is taking care of the trout. Golfing holidays have increased, but they tend to be shorter breaks. The cheap flights bring revellers into Dublin, but these increased numbers don't translate into an awful lot of bed nights around the country.

Irish tourism is more and more dependent on Irish tourists. No one seems to be minding it – promoting it, yes; minding it, no. On a very recent trip to France, I could get a good hotel room for 53 euro in Cherbourg. I did book a hotel in Saint Malo on the Net that was an appalling dump, which cost 39 euro: walked out of the place, went next door and got a fine hotel for 38 euro, lift, en suite, all of those good things. I won't bore you or upset you with other price comparisons – the food, the drink – but it was clear, by and large, the French nurtured their tourism. It was competitive. Prices didn't seem to vary a lot year to year; tourists seemed to be appreciated. And, yes, they have the best cuisine in the world, fine wines at affordable prices. They have got standards.

We have some great restaurateurs, some very competent hoteliers, angling operators, that kind of person, but there are things that *they* can't control. There might come a time, and I hope it's not soon, when tourism equals economic survival, and if it does, we'll have a lot of catching up to do.

Welcome welcome everyone

Broadcast 21 November 2005

Immigration to Ireland is really nothing new, and quite a few of those over the years who came here were fleeing persecution. They were, in effect, asylum-seekers. Near where Baggot Street meets Stephen's Green, you can still see the Huguenot graveyard. These were French Protestants at the time of King Louis who fled the persecution of Catholic France.

Jewish immigration in the nineteenth century was mostly from eastern Europe and tsarist Russia. In the twentieth century, Jews from all over Europe sought refuge here. Too few were granted asylum. Ireland's record in relation to the Jews is not a good one. At the height of the Holocaust, one Dáil deputy asked, 'In view of the efficacious measures being taken by the German Government to deal with the Jewish problem, what steps will Mr de Valera take?' That deputy, by the way, became a cabinet minister in the Labour–Fine Gael coalition from 1973 to 1977.

Italians started coming to Ireland in significant numbers in the 1900s, and after the Second World War, many arrived as economic refugees, mostly from near Monte Casino, which saw some of the most intense fighting of the Allied progress through Italy.

Closer to home, from 1969 onwards, northern nationalists fled the conflict in Belfast, in particular, and were regarded with some suspicion here. Yes, some were fugitive gunmen, but most were just frightened people looking for a safe place to live. It was a paranoid time, when many of the institutions of state paid only lip-service to the notion that we were all Irish and equal.

I remember trying to get back into journalism in 1973 and auditioning for RTÉ Radio to be told in a cultured Dublin drawl that I was, 'very good, but that the voice really doesn't fit this side of the border.' Well, when the owner of the voice left the room, a broad Cork voice in the corner said, 'Pay no attention to him, auld stock, your stuff is great, keep at it.' The Corkman was Donnacha O'Dulaing, and I took his advice to become, at the time, one of perhaps only three northern voices working for RTÉ. There was Frank Hall, Rodney Rice, and there was me.

A new Head of News would employ more Northerners and more women too, by the way. But even in the late 1970s, there were very few northern voices on RTÉ. A colleague, one of our specialist correspondents, and a fine fellow in many ways, complained that there were too many, until I pointed out that two-fifths of the population of this island had some sort of northern accent.

Well, the French Huguenots are long assimilated, and the Jewish population has dwindled, but it made a significant contribution to public life here. Everyone loves the Italians – hard-working, flamboyant, independent – and, whisper it, Northerners are everywhere. No one really seems to mind too much; there are still relatively few northern voices on air, but behind the scenes, let me assure you, no shortage. What I am getting at is that in time, you have, without working at it, come to accept strangers in your midst because, after a while, they, we, have ceased to be strangers.

The past few years of massive immigration pose a special challenge. Acceptance, assimilation, if you like, need help, needs conscious decisions and policies. Michael McDowell is right: we require a mix of gardaí. That's his department. But we need a lot more. Every aspect of life here must be open to new citizens and not blocked by Irish-language requirements or the unwritten religious codes imposed on would-be teachers. We must be an inclusive society: the alternative is anger, fire, death, injustice.

Forty years ago, perhaps more – I was a teenager – 120 brown bodies were fished out of the river Seine in Paris, after just a single night. All those years later, Paris burns, because no one really made the effort. A police force that has alienated young people of colour; 30 per cent unemployment in those ghetto areas; a hard-nosed home-affairs minister; a rapidly polarising society. If some of that seems familiar, think Derry, Strabane, West Belfast in the late 1960s and remember what happened when that anger was harnessed to an ideology.

There must be other voices on RTÉ and on TV3 and on the twenty or so radio stations around the country. There must be gardaí with black or brown complexions, teachers of many religious beliefs, judges in touch with this new Ireland, political parties prepared to practise what they preach, housing – not just for immigrants and not just for native Irish. Housing is a great source of grievance. It's not enough to leave it all to the Department of Justice, not enough to say, 'It will do for the moment.' The alternative is there for all to see, in France.

A difficult and bloody birth

Broadcast 17 February 2006

For eleven years, with Thelma Mansfield, I presented RTÉ 1's daytime television programme *Live at Three*. It was, many of you will recall, a mixture of features, fashions, food and music. And, given a bit of bad weather, to whit a blizzard, we could attract up to a million viewers. UK producers came over to observe and use it as a template for their own daytime programmes.

But there was one strand of programming never copied. Every Monday, an invited audience of older viewers would arrive by bus for lunch and *Live at Three*. They were the show: their lives, their stories. Active retirement groups, community groups, parish organisations. There was a little music, but mostly it was about *them*. Back in the 1980s, there were still many who had memories of 1916, the War of Independence and the Civil War. Some had participated in those events.

Don't believe that time always mellows. I recall the widow of one of Pearse's aides, bitterly snarling, 'The men betrayed us.' When I observed gently that the killing had to stop sometime, she blazed back, 'It stopped too soon.' She was one of very many who still had strong feelings and vivid memories: of the 1916 rebels being cursed and spat on by the Dublin crowd as they were marched off to Frongoch Prison; of British forces dumping a father's body on the steps of his home; of reprisals and counter-reprisals, a spiral of terror, which didn't end with British withdrawal – if anything, it became more savage.

On the seventy-fifth anniversary of the 1916 uprising, we assembled a dozen or fourteen eyewitnesses, people who were in the centre of Dublin that fateful Easter week. There was humour as one man recalled women looting the damaged shops and comparing their booty. There was an extraordinary story of two very drunk British soldiers near Boland's Bakery. A volunteer raised his rifle to kill them, but a tall figure in uniform pushed the gun barrel down and told his subordinate, 'We don't shoot drunks.' Thus, Éamon de Valera saved the lives of two British tommies.

There was confusion or reticence about a lot that went on Easter week, 1916. Most of the surviving witnesses, of course, plumped for support of the uprising, but it's by no means clear that the rebellion was regarded by the majority of Irish people as other than bizarre, an aberration, at that time.

When the next eight years saw the birth of the Irish state, the uprising was vindicated in the public mind. As such, it eclipsed other efforts – the Fenian uprising of 1867 that ended in battles at Stepaside and in Tipperary, almost forgotten. It was estimated by the middle of the nineteenth century that 15,000 Irish soldiers in British regiments had taken the Fenian oath. The men who recruited them were betrayed by Private Patrick Nolan and arrested. These so-called military Fenians narrowly escaped the gallows but were deported on the last prison ship to leave England for New South Wales in Australia to be worked to death. A civilian Fenian who'd escaped from custody and fled to the United States, John Devoy, eventually, with the Irish Republican Brotherhood, organised a daring escape, more spectacular than any work of fiction. The whaling ship *Catalpa* brought them to the United States. President Ulysses S. Grant refused to hand them back to the British. But the revolutionaries hadn't gone away.

To understand the climate of the day by 1916 . . . it's almost impossible for us now. A deal on Home Rule had already been done, fiercely opposed by northern unionists and powerful industrial interests. Ironically, they got Home Rule in the Government of Ireland Act 1920, which, though largely redundant by 1922, became the basis for the Northern Ireland state. 'Home Rule is Rome Rule', they had thundered. They made good and sure that it was never that.

The Fenians' subversion of the British Army, a few decades earlier, scared the unionists. They brought in huge consignments of arms from a helpful Germany. Erskine Childers ran guns into Howth for the Irish Volunteers as a reaction, helped, of course, by a sympathetic Germany.

The debate goes on about the morality of the 1916 uprising. And there were dastardly deeds done by all sides for the next eight years. This state, born out of blood and confusion, was a pretty miserable one for decades to come – an economic invalid, repressed and hypocritical, bereaved by emigration – but not now: wealthy, confident, with the problems of affluence.

Look at some of the other components of the still united kingdom: Scotland, Wales, Northern Ireland, dependent on state subventions from London –

England's poor relations. The revenue from Scotland's oil and whisky going to the British Exchequer; Welsh coal and steel all but gone; Northern Ireland's heavy industry, shipbuilding, engineering (and they were very good), almost wiped out.

If you want to celebrate 1916, celebrate modern, independent – not dependent – Ireland, where, with all its problems, its children can find jobs and its government is representative of the people who elected it. Acknowledge its flaws and try to fix them, but accept the truth, however unpalatable: it had a difficult and bloody birth. Some gave their lives; some took the lives of others; but that was then, and this is now. Accept the past, but live in the present.

The language taliban

Broadcast 26 May 2006

Over the past couple of years, I have written and spoken about lots of things. The North, road safety, the health service, religion and politics, quite a bit more too. As you might expect, not every opinion or conclusion of mine has been met with unanimous approval and universal applause. It's no function of a columnist to endorse a cosy consensus, so I get the odd e-mail demanding that I recant my religious views, modify my political opinions or just keep my nose out of things that are best left to the experts who have made a mess of them in the first place!

But the biggest shower of boulders to come my way wasn't tossed as a result of any of these columns but rather from a slip of the tongue on *Liveline* a couple of years ago, when I referred to TG 'Ceathar' as TG 'Four'. I had used, unintentionally, the English 'four', a kind of shorthand: wrong, but without the intention to offend and in a context, in fact, that was complimentary. But I had polluted an Irish phrase with an English word and had wrongly named TG4.

After about thirty-eight years in journalism, I am well aware of sensitivities, but I was taken aback by the ferocity of the albeit handful of complaints. Although I had a lot of reservations about TG4 when it was first mooted, I think, by Charles Haughey, and then inaugurated by Michael D. Higgins, I am now won over. Having had a lifetime interest in documentaries, I am of the view that some of the very best have been made by and for TG4, and whilst Dublin 4 frequently loses sight of the music and mores of middle Ireland, TG4 doesn't.

My regret is that my Irish isn't up to much, and I have resolved, I admit late in life, to do something about it. That's my decision, just as I kept up a working knowledge of French and toddled off to Spanish night classes. When Paddy Mullen on Inismore puts me in my place in Irish, how I would love to answer him back! I'm enthused, and I want to learn, not because I have to, but because I want to. I don't know why, with such emphasis on Irish in our education system, so few can speak it, but clearly something is wrong with the methodology, a methodology that leaves so many pupils not just unfluent but actively hostile.

My education in the North didn't offer Irish as a subject until second year in secondary school. The alternative was Greek. To my shame, I chose Greek, but those who picked Irish seemed to do pretty well, enjoyed their trips to the Gaeltacht and got good marks in the state exams. There were two Irish teachers: one was a gentle, easy-going priest, the other an enthusiastic batterer, who divided his class into Heaven, Hell and Purgatory. Both seemed to get decent exam results. The one thing that was common to both classes was choice. The pupils had chosen to study Irish.

In the North, Irish was the language of dissent, a way of asserting a national identity despite a determined effort by the Administration to anglicise the education system. Republican prisoners organised language classes in the H-blocks; even the UVF leader Gusty Spence is said to have learned some Irish behind bars, in what they called up there, 'the jailtacht'.

South of the border, a national identity was assumed, and, for many, there was no passion attaching to the language. The language here got no favours either from the zealots who were savage in their abuse of non-Irish speakers. Anyone who had a close encounter with one of them would never be encouraged to learn. I have pondered the great courtesy of native speakers before. Those who inhabited the Nuacht desk during my eleven years in the RTÉ newsroom were amongst the most pleasant and courteous of colleagues, very tolerant of those who lacked their fluency. In contrast, many Dublin-based language enthusiasts, fluent but not native speakers, had a tendency to become rude and aggressive with those who didn't share their enthusiasm.

Irish is a precious part of Ireland's heritage, and it should be nurtured, but it seems to me that the psychology is wrong. Just as Irish flourished in parts of the North because it was almost discouraged officially, the opposite happened here. Some people have no linguistic abilities, just as some, like me, have very few mathematical aptitudes. It's all they can do to scrape by. Now, with all the compulsory Irish, all the extra points, all the extra effort, the traditional approach has not worked. How many fine science teachers have been lost to the state system because their Irish just isn't up to scratch?

Now we are encouraged to embrace a multicultural Ireland. How honest is it to demand a proficiency in Irish for many posts? How much more useful to maintain at least a quota for posts, designated for fluent speakers, not just those who have scraped a pass in their Leaving Cert?

Don't put up barriers, open doors of opportunity. Incentivise, don't compel. Cherish the gaeltachts, resource TG4. If you really care about the Irish language, start thinking about encouraging its use, not compelling it. The Irish psyche reacts adversely to compulsion. You know, if the language had been banned, half the country would now be fluent. That's just the way we are. Whichever way you look at it, it needs another approach, deserves a *better* approach. Now I await the usual hail of stones, but I bet none of the language taliban will be native speakers.

Twenty years a-growing

Broadcast 1 June 2006

RTÉ asked its broadcasters to reflect on the past twenty years. Why just twenty years, I wondered? You see, I'm in my fifties – twenty years seems like a long weekend. Where did it go? Of course, for my sons, twenty years is almost literally a lifetime. And, unlike many countries, we have lots of young people, the cubs who will keep the Celtic Tiger purring, we hope, for at least another generation.

In 1986, RTÉ was developing daytime television. The morning radio ratings were so formidable that television wasn't prepared to compete. (Seems it still isn't!) But the afternoons were different. Radio did not have such an iron grip, and for a couple of years, a little daytime pro-gramme called *Looking Good* had been running an over-fifty-fives talent show. The final pulled 100,000 viewers out of Munster alone.

By and large, the afternoons lost money and had been largely ignored. RTÉ decided to put on something live in the afternoons, some kind of magazine show – small budget, no fanfares, 'look, just get it done'. During one especially nasty bit of weather, the ratings topped 1 million viewers, and, of course, that was key to its success: the availability of viewers – not just those who were retired (only one day a week was aimed at older viewers) but shift workers, housewives, childminders and the unemployed.

When a government department ran a survey to find out the principal source of social-welfare information, *Live at Three* was second only to all of the accumulated print media. You may deduce two things from that: the first is that the programme carried a good, relevant social-welfare slot, and, secondly, lots of people were in receipt of benefits. Unemployment was still very high; fewer mothers were in the labour force. Any item that showed people how to stretch the family budget proved hugely popular. It was touching to see the large number of fathers who wrote in every year approaching Christmas for the plans of our DIY doll's house. You see, in those days, there were many more daddies at home in the afternoons.

Of course, we had our failures: the carefully crafted DIY kennel, for example. A viewer wrote in to say that having installed his peculiarly flatulent hound in our beautiful kennel, he found Fido dead in the morning. We knew the tone was facetious, but why? We checked. We had, of course, omitted any air holes. Sorry, Fido.

An eccentric array of animals appeared. A huge elephant gobbed a gallon and a half of pachyderm snot on my shoulder. It hardened under the lights like plastic; I finished the show like Quasimodo. A pen of famously randy rabbits re-enacted the fall of the Roman Empire, live on air. They still turn up on British television's *It'll Be Alright on the Night*.

By 1990, make-and-do items were dead. It was cheaper to buy clothes from the multiples than to make them, and no one seemed to repair anything any more. The appetite for more exotic, more expensive food was growing. There was evidence that people had more money – not a lot more, but some. Hobby items like oil-painting were growing in popularity. There was an appetite for more expensive and exotic fashion features. Gardening went from propagating your own geraniums to lavish displays of exotic and often expensive plants.

Live at Three moved with the times. It still booked more musical acts, two a day, than anyone else in the business, but now there were more to choose from and more varied. Religion and politics had no part in the programme. The divorce and contraception rows were beyond our remit, but the programme doctor would always break new ground. Incredible though it may seem now, the first graphic discussions on the menopause, breast checks, intimate disorders and much more all took place on *Live at Three*, without, as I recall, a single objection from any viewer. Irish audiences were much more mature than most programme-makers realised.

The show ran for eleven years until 1997, and very few programmes so shrewdly read the economic climate and the changes in society. Some items, and, indeed, maybe this presenter, stayed too long, but we saw the hunger for adult education grow as more and more headed back into the workforce to fill the increasing number of available jobs.

I remember an old man on a Monday show; Mr Bell, I think, was his name. He was in his nineties. An old UVF man, he fought in the trenches alongside the Irish volunteers and spoke warmly of those old comrades, just as he damned the politicians on white horses who saw them off at the railway stations but who never set foot in France or Belgium themselves. Pain, loss and time had granted him clarity, but the later generations had forgotten or never learned those lessons.

I don't know how much *Live at Three* informed society or was informed by society – a bit of both, I suppose – but I know now that the changes that we tracked were the seismic rumblings of an Ireland that was going through the beginnings of an amazing transformation. Mind you, all we were doing was making a programme.

The barbecue bug

Broadcast 19 June 2006

The weather may have changed a bit now, but my local craft butcher had a beatific smile since the good weather began a couple of weeks ago. Hundreds of kilos of his award-winning sausages had been bought in a single weekend, marinated chicken breasts, spare ribs, tons of gold-medal burgers and cubes of meat on skewers – anything, in fact, that can be cooked on a barbecue.

Plumes of smoke rise around the suburbs like harbingers in an Apache uprising. Thousands of barbecues, with all the ancillary equipment, have trundled out of the stores as Irish men prove their machismo by cremating herds of farm animals. For that day, Irish man is American, or Australian, a husky, perhaps a little sooty, outdoors man, because the barbecue is traditionally a male preserve. It's where we take charge. Tongs in one hand, drink in the other, chatting to hungry friends and adoring offspring.

That masculine intrusion into mass family catering can create a bit of a problem. Most Irish men are not accomplished cooks. Those who are tend to be single or married to women who, for all their sterling qualities, never mastered the art of the skillet. There are a few of my acquaintances who make dinner with Lucrezia Borgia a more inviting prospect . . . But back to my generalisations. Women tend to be more fastidious about food –

about food hygiene in particular – and, if they have catered for a young family, they are well aware of the rules about thawing things out, expiry dates and other good practices.

This is the height of the food-poisoning season. The heat means that food left out goes off quickly, and in a fridge packed with the meat for that barbecue, the risk of cross-contamination is great.

There are few more dangerous food occasions than the family barbecue. A while back, I chaired some public meetings for Safe Food, a cross-border semi-state set up after the Good Friday Agreement. You see, someone reckoned that now at least some of the paramilitaries had stopped killing people, it would be nice if the cooks and caterers also reduced their attrition rate. I learned a lot of scary stuff. Food poisoning can and does kill. There are many forms – Campylobacter, Salmonella, E. coli being the best known – and even if you survive, you may have permanent organ damage.

Prudence and good practice will protect you. If you like your burgers pink or red inside, you are literally dicing with death. The juices must run clear, because minced meat has that initial surface contamination mixed all the way through it. A rare steak is probably OK because the surface contamination is killed in the initial searing. Pink pork or poultry is also begging a very close acquaintance with the loo or the intensive-care unit of your nearest acute hospital. Especially for a child or an old person, the consequences can be fatal. Not long ago, E. coli cut a deadly swathe through a Scottish nursing home. You might get away with the kind of food poisoning that settles for vomiting and diarrhoea, but you might not.

A while back, there was a series of ads where anonymous citizens, their faces obliterated by the video editor, confessed their guilt and remorse at having, unwittingly, poisoned family or friends. The ads may have impacted on a few, but the reaction I heard most was a snigger. I pondered that that's perhaps because few realise how dangerous food poisoning is. That's why, when the well-oiled man of the house wields the tongs, he should be reminded that black outside doesn't necessarily mean safe inside. And if oleaginous accompaniments, like coleslaw, are left out of the fridge, they too could be brewing up an epidemic. Mayonnaise, you see, is egg-based and very vulnerable to contamination.

I focused on barbecues because that's when, most often at this time of the year, the unspeakable prepare the uneatable. But the worst bout I ever had was from an ice-cream van – a week later, I was still ill. We had tickets for the Dublin Horse Show. I sat close to the amenities, and if the Irish team had cleared the fences as adroitly as I cleared the seats when the spasms gripped, we would have won the Aga Khan Cup that year.

The law states that everyone, without exception, who handles food commercially must have passed a food-handling course, now available in many languages, but that only applies when you are paying for the food – and do you really believe that all those kids in the forecourt delis have been trained? Still, this time of the year, if you are looking for a really virulent bacterium, barbequing is your best bet.

Putting something back

Broadcast 6 October 2006

The Government's task force on active citizenship has been holding public meetings around the country to find out what motivates people to help those around them for other than personal gain and to identify the things that stop people becoming involved with their community. There is more to it than that, but it struck me how difficult it is to become involved with your community if you spend your life locked in traffic as a commuter. The phenomenon of the ten-hour parent is common – all that's left of the twenty-four-hour day. Our prosperity has come at a high price.

Last week, the day after one such public meeting, well attended and very enlightening, I was in Kinsale for the unveiling of a bronze bust to a man called Peter Barry, not the politician but a retired restaurateur. Remarkably for such an honour, although in poor health, the man was still alive and was guest of honour.[1]

There are those who will say, 'There goes your man Davis banging on about Kinsale again', but there is a point to this. Most will know that Kinsale is a pretty little town, a bit west of Cork city, with a couple of marinas, some fine hotels and a resident population of about

1 Peter Barry died three weeks after the unveiling.

3,000 souls. Yet, there are, by the last count, forty-six places to eat in and around the town. About a dozen form the famous Good Food Circle. It's not an exaggeration to say that the undoubted prosperity of the place is built on its reputation for good food and easy living. Nor is it an exaggeration to say that Peter Barry was the man who started it all.

He'd first seen Kinsale in 1946 as a very young man, and it remained in his heart when he trained in Switzerland as a hotel manager. It stayed in his thoughts even when he was running a fine hotel in the Channel Islands. In 1963, he heard that there was a place for sale in Kinsale, and he bought it. There was only one other restaurant, and that was run by Hedli MacNeice, widow of the poet Louis MacNeice, and, at Peter's suggestion, they referred customers to each other. Other restaurants opened, and Peter coordinated what became the Good Food Circle. There were other seaside towns with restaurants, but none worked together quite so closely or so effectively.

There were twinnings and festivals, including the annual Gourmet Festival (this weekend celebrating its thirtieth anniversary). Even after his retirement from the catering trade, Peter Barry continued to forge links with other towns abroad and to promote the town, where rival restaurateurs are close friends and where energetic young restaurateurs and hoteliers still come to take over from those retiring. The season for most businesses is now twelve months 'long. The restaurants glow in the candlelight. There is laughter and the clink of glasses. Jazz, blues and traditional music can be heard on the evening air.

Some of it might have happened without Peter Barry, but that unique *esprit* that is Kinsale, no: that's down to Peter Barry, one man whose professional and voluntary life transformed a town.

As an example of active citizenship, it's a remarkable account. That's why the idea to erect a bronze likeness to him met with wholehearted support. It's why so many made the effort to be there. Top Irish chef, Derry Clarke, owner of L'Écrivain in Dublin, was there, along with his wife. In despair, his mother had sent the wild young Derry to work and train with Peter, forty years earlier. It was the making of him. As Derry said, 'Everything I have, I owe to you Peter.'

That bronze was an acknowledgement. All around Ireland, there are remarkable men and women, kindly and committed, who have changed for the better the communities in which they live, most in areas a lot less glamorous than the world of haute cuisine. It would be a good idea if, even late in the day, they were acknowledged in some way, while they were still alive to know that we know and appreciate what they have done – that we say 'thank you'.